T0118041

The Queen of
LEMONADE

KIM PONCE

iUniverse, Inc.
Bloomington

Copyright © 2011 by Kim Ponce

All rights reserved. No part of this book may be used or reproduced by any means, graphic, electronic, or mechanical, including photocopying, recording, taping or by any information storage retrieval system without the written permission of the publisher except in the case of brief quotations embodied in critical articles and reviews.

Unless otherwise indicated, Bible quotations are taken from the *Holy Bible, New International Version*. *NIV*. Copyright © 1973, 1978, 1984 by International Bible Society. Used by permission of Zondervan Publishing House. All rights reserved.

Scripture quotations marked CEV are taken from *Contemporary English Version,* Copyright © 1995 American Bible Society. All rights reserved.

Scripture quotations marked NCV are taken from the *New Century Version*. Copyright © 2005 by Thomas Nelson, Inc. Used by permission. All rights reserved.

iUniverse books may be ordered through booksellers or by contacting:

iUniverse
1663 Liberty Drive
Bloomington, IN 47403
www.iuniverse.com
1-800-Authors (1-800-288-4677)

Because of the dynamic nature of the Internet, any Web addresses or links contained in this book may have changed since publication and may no longer be valid. The views expressed in this work are solely those of the author and do not necessarily reflect the views of the publisher, and the publisher hereby disclaims any responsibility for them.

ISBN: 978-1-4502-8130-0 (sc)
ISBN: 978-1-4502-8131-7 (hc)
ISBN: 978-1-4502-8132-4 (ebook)

Printed in the United States of America

iUniverse rev. date: 01/06/2011

Dedication

I dedicate this book to my husband Michael
who lifts me up and keeps me smiling.

Table of Contents

Acknowledgments

There are so many people who helped me through the treatments as well as through getting this book published. For years my mother has encouraged me to write a book. So I need to start with her. Thank you, Mom! You are the most patient, creative, encouraging mom in the world. I wouldn't be the person I am today without all you did for me and all that you taught me. I also want to thank my dad, who never let me think that anything was impossible, doesn't take excuses and is the most generous person I know. Thank you, Dad, for helping to mold me into the woman I have become. Thank you for your wisdom along the way. My brother Andrew was one of my great encouragers during the treatment. Andrew, your success at overcoming adversity has inspired me for years. I am proud to have you as my friend and as my brother. My dear sister Merridith, you are always there for me no matter what. I am blessed to have you as my best friend.

My husband Michael is the best husband in the world even when I am not the best wife in the world. He never complained during the treatments and all of the extra work that piled on him. He encouraged me in the writing and rewriting of this book. I love you, Michael, this much and more and forever and ever. I should thank my boys, Michael and Alex, who keep me smiling and work so hard. You all make me a better person, a better advocate and a better mom.

I would like to give a special thanks to my father-in-law, Dr. Lou Ponce, for putting up with me and for trying to guide me on the right path. Thank you to my mother-in-law who hung out with me when I didn't have the energy to go places. Thank you also to my stepmom,

Nancy, who continually offers me encouragement in all things. A big hug of thanks to my stepdad, Frank, who always shows his love, always listens and sends me the latest information.

My little circle of friends who started on this saga with me deserve a lot of the credit as they lifted me up on a weekly basis and helped me laugh at my mistakes. So a big hug and even bigger thank you to Jill and Russ, Vandana and David, Patty and Ernie. I am also grateful for my many cousins who prayed for me, let me stay with them and helped me keep my attitude positive. Thank you especially, Lauren, Carrie and Yvonne. Thank you also to Helena for your smiles and encouragement. I am grateful for Lori B. who helped my children to be their best. My deepest gratitude to Cheryl for getting my hair back to normal. A big hug to my dear friends Amy and Angelica who keep me going every week.

There will always be a place in my heart for my Acts 2:42 class at Connell. Thank you especially, Gary, Sally, Karen, Lanny, Leanne, Frank, and George. Thank you for all my new friends at St. Tim's who took the torch without even knowing it. There are so many to thank I don't know where to begin. Kristi and Jill welcomed me in. PF, Susie, Judy, Joline, Monica, Shirley, and Pastor Groce kept me going. I need to give a big thank you to Bill and the rest of the VBS staff for bringing joy to my life. I almost forgot a big hug for the Tennessee Cousins who filled in as my local family. I apologize if I forgot to mention anyone. I was truly lifted up by so many people along the way. I am very blessed.

Finally, I want to thank, Kay, Amy, Tammy and Kyle for their publishing advice and Renee Fuqua of Fuqua Photography for her beautiful cover art and author photo.

Preface

Dear Reader,

What would you do if you found out that you had a potentially fatal disease, and that it had already damaged part of your liver? What if the only treatment for the disease was long and difficult? And only 50 percent of the people were cured? Those were the questions I faced.

What would you do?

I have a family that I love and a God who loves me. I didn't have to start treatment. I didn't show any outward signs of illness. But a person has only one liver. I also believed that God would take my experience and show me how to help others from it. So I chose to start forty-eight weeks of antiviral therapy to reduce and possibly eliminate Hepatitis C from my body.

Was it easy? Not always. Was my family infected? No. Was my family affected? Absolutely. Did I want to quit? Yes. Did I forget how to smile and have a good time? Never. Did God bless me during this time? Every week. I shared my story in weekly emails to my family, so in many ways this is a photo journal of my treatment as well as the lessons learned.

God blessed me when he opened my eyes and my heart in new ways. I have an incredible sense of joy that God has given me. I want to share that joy with you. May God bless you and keep you and make his face to shine upon you and give you the ability to take the bitters of life, add some sweetness and stir.

Sincerely,

The Queen of Lemonade

Part 1

—∞∞∞—

Blessed at Birth

Chapter 1

Blessed from Birth

"I am your creator. You were in my care even before you were born."
Isaiah 44:2 CEV

AWAITING HEART TRANSPLANT OPERATION

Kimberly Ann Raquet, daughter of Walter
and Kristine Raquet is still a patient in
Meadowbrook Hospital. The surgeons are
now awaiting a donor in order to perform
a heart transplant. Kimberly Ann will be
four months old on July 5th. Let us all
remember her and her young parents, as
well as her grandparents, in our prayers.

(From the bulletin July 7. 1968 –Christ the King Lutheran
Church in New York)

In what can only be described as the mistake that may have saved
my life, my mother told the nurses that I was allergic to everything
except for bananas. The nurses fed me peaches, the night before my
operation. I broke out in hives, which began to bleed and became
infected causing the doctors to cancel my heart surgery. (I don't recall

any successful heart transplant surgeries until years later.) God does not always give us what we pray for but he ultimately knows better.

THANKS

The Raquet family wishes to extend their sincere thanks and appreciation to all who have been remembering Kimberly Ann Raquet (infant daughter of Kristine and Walter Raquet) in their prayers. God has been good, and the doctors feel that Kimberly is progressing so well that an operation will not be necessary. They feel that she may outgrow her heart condition. She is gaining slowly, but is a happy and alert little girl, who wins the hearts of all who see her. We offer our thanks to God, and ask that you pray that she will continue to "grow in strength, wisdom and stature with God."

(From our church bulletin September 1, 1968-Christ the King Lutheran Church in New York)

Just before my sixth birthday, my parents were told that I needed open heart surgery. They were informed that if I didn't have it, I would probably only live a couple of years. With the surgery, there was a 60 percent chance that I would live to adulthood. They waited until just after my birthday before they checked me into the New York University Medical Center.

My parents tried to prepare me for the hospital stay. They told me it was like a giant pajama party. I was in the hospital for three weeks in April of 1974. My parents lived in East Northport on Long Island. They had to travel two hours into New York City to visit me. My younger brother was not quite five and my little sister Merridith was now two and a half so they were not allowed to visit.

Doctors Spencer and Reed performed two surgeries on me that same day that had never been performed together. One surgery was to correct a mitral valve that was staying open instead of opening and closing. Because the valve had stayed open so long, I had an adult size heart at age six. They also had to add in a missing portion of my aorta artery. They would use one of the other arteries from my body. The surgery lasted fourteen hours, they had to refill my body twice with blood. Dr. Spencer would eventually publish a record of my surgery in a major medical journal. The day of the surgery it took eight nurses to hold me down to give me a shot. For years, I would despise the smell of rubbing alcohol and shots. My church held a twenty-four-hour prayer vigil for me. I still have the sign up sheet.

The surgery went well. I was in the recovery room after the surgery when I sat up pulled out my breathing tubes and said, "You are all fired because I missed Carrie's birthday party." They immediately got my tubes situated. My mother almost passed out upon hearing the news. My cousin Carrie's birthday is April 11. Although I did miss her birthday party, my parents snuck Carrie and my brother Andrew in through a freight elevator. I still remember the tears in my eyes as I greeted them. When I was in recovery, members of my church visited me and gave me a sack filled with toys. The people at my dad's office chipped in and bought me a small black and white television.

Eventually, I returned home and recovered. I began to thrive. I no longer needed medicine for my heart. Every year, I had to take the train into the city to see my pediatric cardiologist, Dr. Eugenie Doyle. I still remember holding my mom and dad's hands as they helped me step onto the Long Island Railroad. After the visit, we would have lunch at a fancy restaurant in the city. I went every year for a long time and then every two years. I don't remember anything about my recovery at home.

My final visit was when I was in college. Dr. Doyle thought I should undergo a stress test to see if my heart was strong enough to have children someday. At the time, that was the furthest thing from my mind. So I sat there waiting in a room full of children wondering if I would be able to have my own someday. It had never occurred to me that I might not be able to. At a later date, I came into the city again to have my first Thallium Stress Test done. It consisted of my walking on a treadmill as they increased the incline and the speed while I had a needle stuck in my arm. At one point they injected the radioisotope thallium into my bloodstream. I joked the whole time with the techs saying it was like shopping when there was a sale at Macy's and the store was about to close. After the injection, they let me cool down, while they watched the dye move around my heart. My prognosis was great. Now I just had to finish college, get married and have kids.

Growing up in New York on Long Island, I never would have guessed I would someday settle down in Tennessee. I met my husband while I was in college. I debated for Emerson College in Boston. He debated for Suffolk University in Boston. We first met at a tournament held at Ithaca College in upstate New York. My coach introduced us. Michael has the biggest smile you have ever seen. Whenever he saw me he would smile. Two years later he asked me out and the rest is history.

We were married in 1992. Michael graduated from Tulane Law School in 1993 and we moved to Tennessee just outside of Nashville so that Michael could open his own law practice. In 1999, we had our first son Michael Augustus. In 2001 we had our second son Alexander. They are healthy, energetic, funny and smart. In other words . . . a handful. One is quiet. One can't stop talking. They both love to travel and they get along pretty well for being brothers. My in-laws come to visit us about once a week. The kids call them Mama Bear and Pop Pop. The kids call my mom and her husband: Mama Tina and Grandpa Frank. And my dad and his wife are called Grandpa Walter and Grandma Nancy. So now you have met a good part of my family.

And here I am thirty some odd years later to tell you about how God changed my life again. Back in the winter of 1996, I had started with a different Sunday school class. This class seemed to know everything about the Bible and God. I immediately let them know I was in Bible Kindergarten comparatively. They loved me anyway. One day after a particularly good service and class I said a prayer. I prayed that I could get closer to God. I desired that strong relationship that others in my class seem to possess. I already had a very strong faith from all that I had gone through as a child. Now it was time to get closer to God and take my relationship to a new level.

Chapter 2

Diagnosis

On September 11, 2001, when the Twin Towers (the World Trade Center) collapsed after having been hit by terrorist piloted airplanes, I watched in horror with the rest of the world. My father had once worked at Cantor Fitzgerald (one of the firms on the top floor.) He lost forty people he knew on that day. My great-grandfather, Julius Sjulin, a Swedish immigrant had been an ironworker for Bethlehem Steel. He had worked on the Twin Towers on the basement floors just before he had retired.

I thought about donating blood during the aftermath of the disaster but the lines were so long and my son Alex was just a baby. About five or six months later, I was visiting my husband's office and saw a Red Cross bloodmobile parked out front and thought, "AHA! This is perfect. Now I can give blood." So I filled out the paperwork, gave blood and happily left knowing that I had done something.

Several weeks later I received a letter in the mail from the Red Cross stating that they were unable to use my blood because it had antibodies for hepatitis C. I couldn't believe it. I looked it up on my computer and was quickly horrified about the silent killer hepatitis C. I told my husband when he came home. He called his dad who is a doctor. My father-in-law suggested that I probably picked up the disease from my blood transfusions during my open-heart surgery when I was six years old. What irony that the surgery that saved my life was now the source of a potentially fatal disease! But I know God has a plan, a purpose for me.

My father-in-law suggested that we run a liver function test to see if the disease damaged my liver. Hepatitis C can hide in your system for years without producing a single symptom. It can attack your liver and then stop and go into hiding again. The treatments listed on the Internet give you flu-like symptoms, make your hair fall out and lots of other unpleasant stuff. My husband and my children were tested for the disease and they were negative. My liver function test came back normal. So my father-in-law recommended that we test it every six months and that I should stop drinking alcohol and stop taking Tylenol.

So I did. Nothing happened. Eventually, I had a glass of wine every now and then. So for the next four years nothing else happened. I even convinced myself that I didn't have the disease, just the antibodies for it.

Summer 2006

Then one hectic Friday before Memorial Day Weekend in 2006, I was speaking with my father-in-law about our plans for the weekend, when he started talking about some articles he read about using chemo to treat patients with Hepatitis B. I was confused. I said, "But Pop Pop, I don't have the disease, I just have the antibodies." He said, "No. You have the disease." He proceeded to tell me that I should probably have more testing done. I was so furious. I hung up the phone on him. Then I called my husband and began sobbing into the phone, all the while trying not to let my kids see me upset.

My husband raced home and listened while I relayed the conversation. He called his father back. He reassured me that nothing new had shown up on my recent blood work. We decided to consult a liver expert. Almost a month later I met my new gastroenterologist at Vanderbilt University Medical Center. We will call him Dr. Mike. After I waited for an hour in the patient room, he came in. He asked me a bunch of questions and asked me if I had any questions. He also explained how hepatitis C worked. He told me the disease itself is not what kills you. It is your immune system attacking the disease, which causes the disease to make scar tissue to protect itself. This scar tissue is called cirrhosis of the liver (scarring of the liver). So if your immune system doesn't mind it being there, it can live in your system, literally for years. I explained that since I am not an IV drug user and had not prostituted myself that I probably received the disease through the blood transfusion during my open-heart surgery.

"So what do we do now?" I asked. He said, "Well, first we have to determine which type it is. There are three types in the US: Geno Types 1, 2 and 3. Types 2 and 3 have an 80 percent chance of being cured through six months of antiviral therapy. Genotype 1 is what most people have and it is only 40-50 percent curable with 12 months of antiviral therapy." He also wanted to determine how active the virus had been and to see if there had been any damage to my liver. So I had to have a blood test and then pending the results go for a liver biopsy. If I had Type 2 or 3, he said he would highly recommend going on to the antiviral therapy. He also suggested that I get a CT scan of my liver to get a gross picture. I felt good meeting Dr. Mike. I felt relief in that now I had a plan of action. I stopped off to have my blood drawn and headed home.

I have always been bossy, aggressive and a bit of a control freak. I am the kind of person that gets things done. The way I deal with stress is I always have a plan. Sometimes I even have a plan B and a plan C. I find if I have a plan, a strategy for addressing a problem then I can stop worrying about it and go on with my life. So I don't generally get anxious about things. I just make a plan.

A week later, my husband watched the kids while I went for a CT scan of my liver. It was quick and easy, not painful other than the prick of a needle in my arm in order to run an IV. During a CT scan, they lay you down flat, place an IV in your arm and tell you to raise your arms above your head while you gently slide into what looks like the center of a metal donut. A special dye is injected into your body through the IV, which makes you feel extremely hot for a minute or two. They ask you to hold your breath. Lights on the donut whirr around like a carnival game. Before you know it the technician says 'breathe" and you are backed out, disconnected and free to go.

I had called Dr. Mike's office earlier in the week to find out the results of my blood tests. My cholesterol, white blood cell count and liver enzymes and such were all normal. The hepatitis C count (known as the viral load) was over 3,500,000. I asked the nurse what was normal. She seemed surprised and said zero was normal. "Oh, of course," I said. It would still be another week before I found out which type I had. I asked her to call me when she knew. I got the call a week later on a Friday. She told me I had Type 1 hepatitis C. She told me the doctor would write me a follow-up letter, but he was going on vacation so it would be two weeks before I probably received it.

So I had the information I needed . . . the dreaded Type 1, harder to cure than the others, a year of antiviral therapy (that only cures half of those who complete the treatment.)

Two weeks later on a Monday morning, I was scheduled for a biopsy. I was feeling ok about it, not really afraid. Mostly I just wanted to know more information about how my liver was faring.

Dr. Mike explained that he would insert an instrument into my liver and it would extract a small sample of my liver. He also explained that sometimes people felt pain somewhere else on their body instead of the liver. Once they examined the liver they would know if any damage had been caused, which would help me to decide whether or not to get treatment.

Soon they had inserted the special tool for taking a nick out of my liver. The doctor told me he was about to do it. OW! It felt like he had sucker punched me. It was horrible because now I was about to cry and felt nauseous. My right shoulder also hurt for some reason. The doctor left with his sample as I watched him through teary eyes. I asked one of the nurses to get my friend, Vandana, who brought me. Eventually, she was allowed back in. I felt such relief seeing her so I let her distract me. Then I tried to rest. Later on she brought me home and stayed for a while. I felt much better.

On Thursday, I received a call from the nurse at Dr. Mike's office saying they had the results of the biopsy. I had stage 2 inflammation and stage 2 scarring of the liver. So the next morning, I sat waiting for Dr. Mike a little bit less calm than the last time, wondering what my future would be.

Chapter 3

My Future Revealed

Dr. Mike told me that my liver had stage 2(out of 4) scarring of the liver and stage 2 inflammation. My viral count was high too. So the disease had affected my liver. Dr. Mike explained my options: I could start on antiviral therapy, which consisted of Ribivirin pills every day and once a week shots of pegylated interferon. I would be on the therapy for forty-eight weeks even if the virus cleared within the first month. The side effects include: flulike symptoms, fevers, aches and pains, hair loss (Dr. Mike said it was more like hair thinning), abdominal pain, diarrhea, depression, loss of energy, nausea and more. I began to tear up. I started thinking of my son Alex who had just started kindergarten. I thought of being too weak to help out in his class. I thought of missing field trips. It was too much and I started to sob. I didn't want to miss out on all of Alex's firsts. I had been at most of Michael's field trips and had scrap booked his entire kindergarten year.

Dr. Mike handed me his tissue box. He told me that I didn't have to start the treatment. Instead, we could do follow-up viral count tests every so often and put it off and maybe have a biopsy every three to five years. There were other drugs that were not approved yet but would begin trials soon. I started to calm down then I asked him, "OK, here is the $25,000 question! Knowing what you know, what would you do if you were in my shoes?" He said, "You only have one liver. So I would probably go ahead with the antiviral therapy." He then told me how the therapy was easier for people who were already healthy. He also mentioned that some people are super responders. Eighty percent of the super responders clear the virus entirely. He also told me that one of his patients had finished his forty-eight weeks that morning. He had cleared the virus and had told Dr. Mike that the side effects hadn't been too bad. So I told him I would have to think about it.

I called my husband and he met me at home and we talked over lunch. My husband grew up around the medical field. His father is a surgeon and his mother is a nurse. He worked in a nursing home before getting his bachelor's degree in biology. He had been a pre-med student before he received his MBA and finally studied law. So I value his opinion not only as my husband and my best friend but also as someone who has some knowledge in the area. He felt that it was my decision but agreed with Dr. Mike. I mentioned that I didn't have to start the treatment right away. I began to think . . . Perhaps I could start it after Christmas, so that way I could get through the Christmas holiday this year while I was still strong and be finished a couple of weeks before next Christmas. That way I would be taking back some control over the situation. I figured everyone gets the flu in the winter, so my side effects would seem normal. I would be done in time for the next Christmas and then have all of the drugs out of my system in time to celebrate my fortieth birthday in March of 2008. So, I could celebrate with a great big party and not worry about being sick. OK, the decision was made. I could live with that. Just one thing . . . I needed to check with my cardiologist. I wanted to make sure that my heart was strong enough to take the antiviral therapy.

So, I was able to see my cardiologist, Dr. Ben, the following week. He said my heart was doing fine. He was happy that I was exercising. He said I was good to go. But the following week, I received a call that he had reviewed my last stress thallium test and saw something odd that would normally be nothing but with stress it could be a problem. So in order to take a better look he scheduled a CT scan of my heart. A week later, his nurse called me back and said that my insurance wouldn't pay for a CT scan so he was scheduling me for a catheter procedure. I didn't know what that was. She explained that you get checked in early, and they run a tube through your groin area up to the heart to see how things are going. Then after the procedure, you have to remain still for four or more hours and maybe stay overnight. The reason that I had to get a catheter was due to the fact that in 1974 when they performed the surgery they used metal clips. The doctors were unable to see through them to examine the suspect area. So I set up the catheter procedure to happen the day after Halloween.

Upon hearing the news, my mom and stepdad Frank called me to say that they could come for a week and be there for the procedure. They arrived the day before Halloween. The night before the procedure, I thought some extra protection wouldn't be a bad idea. So I sent out the following email to my Sunday School Class:

From: Kim Ponce
Sent: Tuesday, October 31, 2006
To: Moore, Gary
Subject: prayer request

Dear Gary:

Tomorrow I will be at Vanderbilt to have a catheter procedure done on my heart. The story is too long to tell. They have discovered a widening of one of my arteries just past a metal clip that has been there since I was 6 years old when I had my open-heart surgery. My cardiologist told me it could be nothing or it could be some type of blockage that is causing blood to pool in that area. I am scheduled to have the procedure done at 11:45 AM and I will have to lie still for 4-6 hours after the procedure to make sure that everything heals well. If they do discover a blockage they will work to remove it and I will have to stay overnight. I am blessed that my mother decided last week to make plans to surprise me and come for a week-long visit this week. She and my stepdad Frank arrived safely from NJ yesterday. Thank you.

Sincerely,

Kim Ponce

The next day as Mom and Frank took me to the admissions office at the hospital, I was surprised and delighted to see Pastor Glass and Chris Kearney from church waiting for me in the lobby. They had gotten my email and I had scared them half to death. I broke down and explained half of the story, then I was called back to fill out forms so my mom took over for me. They prayed for me and headed back to church. Pastor Glass called several times during the day to check in on me. My appointment had been for 10:00 AM, but because there were more serious heart patients that needed the procedure, they were added into the schedule. I didn't go back until after 6:00 PM They shaved my groin, where the catheter was going in. Even though they did it in a very polite manner, I couldn't help wondering what it must be like for some little old lady to have that done. How shocking and scary it would be. This was my first gift of empathy.

I was finished after 8:00 PM and I was allowed to eat finally. I was then checked into a room to stay overnight for observation. I had not planned on this. I had hardly slept at all between pain and the nurses waking me up every two to three hours to weigh me and check my temperature, etc. By 5:30 AM I had threatened the nurse that I would take out the IV if she didn't. I have never been patient. I almost took a cab home but I didn't have my wallet. All of my personal things except my clothes had been sent home with Mom and Frank. I called my husband at 6:00 AM, waking him up. I wanted to break out of jail. He had to get the boys ready and get them to school. He said he would come for me after they discharged me. (My husband is my voice of reason most of the time. I hate it when he is right.)

They wouldn't discharge me without first having me see the cardiologist who had performed the catheter procedure. I was about to hit the ceiling. I just wanted to go home. I wanted to sleep. The doctor arrived about an hour later. He was very nice to me and explained why he had wanted me to stay overnight. He wanted to make sure that I didn't have any complications. So he signed off on my papers. I called my husband and stomped toward the elevator. I got in the elevator and felt weak and stupid knowing I probably should have stayed in bed. But being impatient is one of my weaknesses.

So I sat in the lobby and waited for my husband. I was wiped out for a day and a half. I couldn't lift my children and I felt fragile. The irony is I went through this to find out if I was strong enough to go through antiviral therapy. And I was. Yippee? I think.

I spent the next weeks seeing family and friends and enjoying the Christmas season. I even had our first ever World Peace Dinner Party. It was a lot of fun with dishes from all over the world. All of the Christmas activity kept my mind off of January. I did have to set my medicine up. Apparently, the medicines for antiviral therapy are not available at the local Walgreens. You have to sign up with special pharmacies that mail the prefilled syringes and pills to your doorstep. As I began to investigate, I found out the medicine for the forty-eight weeks of treatment would cost over $24,000 dollars. I was at a loss for words. Luckily, I kept calling around until someone suggested I call my insurance company and find out what they covered. I found out that once I met my deductible it would be mostly covered. Phew! Now I wondered how anyone without good insurance would ever be able to afford the treatment. The pharmaceutical companies have some financial aid programs but still. . . .

January arrived and it was time to begin antiviral therapy. My family lives out of state so I tried to keep them updated by email with pictures so they wouldn't worry too much. I tried to let them know about what I felt God was teaching me along the way.

Part 2

—◦◦◦—

My Spiritual Journey during Treatment

But blessed is the man who trusts in the Lord,
whose confidence is in him.
He will be like a tree planted by the water
that sends out its roots by the stream.
It does not fear when heat comes;
its leaves are always green.
It has no worries in a year of drought
and never fails to bear fruit. Jeremiah 17:7-8

January 3, 2007 7:43 AM

Dear Friends and Family:

This isn't my best look, but I recently had pink eye and have not been wearing a lot of makeup. Well, tomorrow I start the very first treatment. I have the medicine in my fridge already. In the morning, I will meet with Anna, the nurse who coordinates the people receiving treatments and she is going to show me how to give myself a shot. Here is where my experience with giving allergy shots to my dog and testing myself for sugar when I had gestational diabetes should help. The effect of the shot will be delayed by several hours so it shouldn't begin to affect me until nighttime. I don't feel apprehensive. I guess mostly I feel as though I will feel better once I go through a week of treatment to know how it will affect me so that I can plan. Mom and Frank arrive on Saturday to help out for a week. I am hoping that I won't need help and we can go shopping and decorate instead. Keep me in your prayers. I will send you an update soon.

Kim

January 4, 2007 7:49 AM

Well, I got through the first day. Drinking water is supposed to reduce the side effects. So I have been pouring down water all day long. It is currently 7:44 PM.I felt a little chilled an hour ago but I am better now. The nurse gave me Tylenol to take before I gave myself the shot and I also had Motrin this afternoon.

I have also taken my Ribivirin pills. So far the only side effect was nausea when my husband breathed near me. He had eaten sardines and crackers with his dinner. Well, I am going to settle down for the night and take it easy. Thank you for the prayers.

Love,

Kim

January 4, 2007 9:27 PM

Thank you for all of your prayers. I feel great. Last night I did run a fever while I was trying to sleep but it came and went. So I got lots of sleep and no aches and pains. I woke up this morning feeling like Superwoman. I was so filled with relief that it gave me energy. I did everything I normally do this morning including drive the kids to school. I feel like I am going to be just fine. It helps that I have the support of my family and friends.

Love you,

Kim

January 11, 2007 5:00 AM

Hey Everyone (my small circle of confidants):

I have made it through the first week of treatment (only 47 more to go.) Woo hoo! I have kept up my massive water intake, which seems to help with the side effects. Mostly I am getting tired faster. Sometimes I have a little bit of nausea. The only weird side effect I have had is that sometimes I feel like someone has a voodoo doll of me and is using a staple gun on my head. It all happens very quickly so it is not like a headache. Mom and Frank have spoiled me this week. They have been cooking, doing laundry and entertaining the kids and us. We have also had fun. I believe my mother may have half of New Jersey praying for me. Once again, I thank you for your prayers. God is awesome. I have injected myself again today and hopefully the fever will start at bedtime again like last week. My antiviral therapy is supposed to get rid of disease in 40-50 percent of the people who take it. My doctor told me that some people are super responders to the medicine and they have miraculous results right away. About 80 percent of those people are cured of the disease. I know God has a plan for me in all of this.

Love to all,

Kim

January 11, 2007 11:43 PM

Yeah. I made it through another Thursday. This time was a little bit worse with the fever/nausea and fatigue but I'm good.

Have a great weekend, everyone.

Love,

Kim

January 15, 2007 8:35 PM

Hello Everyone:

I have realized that I need to put myself first although as a mom that is difficult to do. I haven't stayed as hydrated as last week and I didn't take my pills on time yesterday so I have had insomnia, nausea and muscle stiffness the last two mornings. Kind of the way you feel the day after you work out. So today I will become organized. I am finding it hard to remember to do things and that is screwing up my week too. Oh, and Michael Augustus needs glasses. He was not happy about it. I will pick them up today. The good news is they are a lot less expensive than I remember my glasses being (before lasik). Thank you for your ongoing prayers; it is helping. I am just off schedule after being spoiled by Mom and Frank last week. My mom said in my last picture I looked scared so I hope you see this picture and think I look determined.

Love,

Kim

January 18, 2007 5:02 AM

Ok. Two weeks down only forty-six to go. The nurse had told me the first couple of weeks are the hardest. So hopefully this is as bad as it gets. On the positive side, I have lost two pounds. I just gave myself my third shot, this time in the leg instead of my belly. (I didn't know there was a positive use for belly fat. But there is. You can hardly feel the shot at all. It just itches like a mosquito bite.) So far I have only gotten sick (bathroom sick) once due to the fact that I didn't have enough food with my medicine. The newest side effect for me is being weepy. One of the side effects is depression. I am not prone to getting depressed so instead it is making me very emotional and weepy, which I can't stand. I hardly ever cry and so this drives me crazy. I get occasional pains like now. It feels like someone has a voodoo doll of me and is trying to sit on my head. It just stopped. Thank you for your continuing prayers.

Love,

Kim

January 18, 2007 6:55 PM

Hey All:

Bad night. I tried to take the shot later so it would start later and it started at 8:30 PM So I attempted to sleep through the fevers until 11:30 PM Then I was awake and could not get back to sleep. I spent the first part of the night up watching TV, working on a puzzle, reading a good book and the second half lying in bed with my eyes closed fully aware of my surroundings until the kids came in at 6 this morning. I think it was a combination of eating half a slice of really rich chocolate cake yesterday at lunchtime (my medicine makes caffeine 8 x more powerful.) and taking my Ribivirin around 5 PM Well, no rest for the weary. Tonight we are celebrating Michael's birthday with a friend sleeping over. At least by noon tomorrow it will be over and I can recover the rest of the weekend.

I don't mean to complain at all. I guess I am just trying to give you a small picture of what I am going through each week. I know God has a plan for me in all of this. I mean I have already experienced getting a heart catheter and now my heart goes out to people who have to have that done. Also, if my insurance did not cover my medicine it would cost $1800 for every four weeks. My heart goes out to those without good insurance.

Thank you my friends and my family for lifting me up.

Love,

Kim

PS I have been reading a series of books by Kathy Herman, a Christian writer. They have all been pretty good.

January 21, 2007 9:06 PM

Good Morning.

I finally got a full night sleep. And I feel great. I broke down and told my Sunday School class about what I am going through. But I asked them to keep it confidential. It was so good to get that off my chest. I have never been good at lying and never really wanted to be. Tomorrow we celebrate Michael Augustus turning eight.

Love,

Kim

Sunday School Confession

The Acts 2:42 class had become a great place for me to learn about the Bible. We always started our class by asking for prayer concerns, then we prayed as we felt led. So there would be silence and different people would pipe up and pray for someone. That morning I couldn't take holding my secret in anymore. I prayed out loud for God to give me the strength to tell the truth. I then slowly began sobbing until I was heaving with sobs. Two of my friends in the class, Karen and Leanne, got up and sat on either side of me, holding me while I continued to sob. My shoulders were heaving, my body was shaking. Our prayer session ended and I said, "I guess I should explain." So I did. I also asked them to keep it a secret and not to ask me how I was doing at church. I didn't want the kids to overhear. I was afraid people would talk about me (out of concern hopefully) and not see one of my children or one of their friends standing nearby listening. My class all agreed to keep it a secret. Then Karen asked if they could pray over me. So I sat on a chair in the middle of the room and everyone placed their hands upon my shoulders or head, and they prayed for me. I thought I would feel embarrassed but instead I felt special and grateful.

January 24,2007 8:33AM

Hi Everyone,

Thank you for your continued prayers. Today is the last day of the first three weeks. This past week I learned to deal with insomnia.

On Monday night, I couldn't sleep until 3:00 AM and then woke up at 6:00 AM when the kids woke up. It was Michael Augustus's birthday so I knew I couldn't sleep in. Later in the day, I was speaking to my good friend Russ and he suggested that I pray, "Thank you God for giving me a good night sleep" even if I didn't have a good night sleep. So I did pray that several times that afternoon and I slept all night. I felt so refreshed. I also found out yesterday that between June, when I was first tested for my HEP C viral load (the amount you have in your body), it was over three million and the day I started the treatment, January 4, it was over four million. So I think I have made a good decision in pursuing treatment.

They will test my blood again mid-February when I go for my doctor's appointment. Another positive note: I had decided that I shouldn't be around lots of children in a closed environment, so I stopped volunteering on Thursdays in Alex's class but I have figured out that I can go to lunch with him instead. He wants me to come every day now. The boys also surprised me this morning and were scrubbing my bathroom tiles for me. They had caught me scrubbing the tile in a different bathroom this weekend and had wanted to help so I showed them how to do it. They did a pretty good job.

Well, good night.

Love,

Kim

January 31, 2007 8:26 A.M

So there! I made it through week four. This week was crazy. I started with a faulty syringe, so I had to take another whole dose of interferon on Saturday. So I have been fatigued and nauseous for days. I didn't write earlier because who really wants to hear about that. But I am a trooper. Monday was horrendous but hilarious. See below if I haven't already told you. The temperature here is dropping rapidly; they expect snow and school closings. However, this morning as I left Panera heading to Trickett Honda to have my transmission replaced, I was freezing. I looked beside me and there sat my hat (now the chicken hat: you see on Monday I purchased chicken nuggets for the kids as an after school snack at Chik-Fil-A. Once I bought the nuggets I thought, How am I going to keep these warm for twenty minutes until we pick up the older kids. I noticed my hat. Aha! I had a great idea. Place the hat over my chicken nugget bag and the fleece would keep it warm. It worked like a charm.) So now as I sat there freezing in the car I picked up the hat and smelled it. Yep, still smelled like chicken. Which means my head would smell like chicken nuggets. After an agonizing two minutes, I donned my chicken hat and drove the rest of the way to Trickett Honda hoping they would not smell me as I got out of the van. Don't worry. I am washing it tonight. And I will probably shower tomorrow to get any residual essence of chicken nugget out of my hair.

My bigger mistake was later today when I was once again at Chik-Fil-A (which has the only indoor play area in case you are thinking I've got a thing for chicken). Today, after I picked up Alex, we met his friend there for a play date. I didn't want to seem like a pill popping mama, so while his friend and his mom went to the bathroom I took a couple of sips of milk shake, downed my pills and started sucking down the rest of it as fast as I could. So it will be a bathroom night for me. But on a positive note, Michael Augustus is pulling his grades back up (see story below). Right now Michael Augustus is reading his brother their bedtime story for me. I helped out in the library on Tuesday and helped organize books in Michael's teacher's class today, had lunch with Alex today too. The boys seem to be happy to see me helping out at school again. I had pulled away from all of that fearing that I would catch an illness since the medicine I am on suppresses my immune system. So I have the sniffles but I will be just fine. Once again, thank you for all of your prayers.

Love to all,

Kim

OK. Here is what happened Monday night:

First, we start off with the fact that my son got glasses two weeks ago and is refusing to wear them in school. Then we have the fact that because he is not wearing glasses he can't see the board, so he is not doing work in Spanish, and music and his own class. If he continues he will go from straight A's to F's. Add on top of this a homework assignment to write, bind and illustrate their own book, which is due in two weeks. By the way, boys do not like to write stories--that would be girls. So we come home after Kumon last night and Michael Augustus makes a lot of progress on his weekly homework pack. I speak to his teacher about coming in to observe in class so I can figure out what to do. Husband calls, feeling on the verge of a cold, is coming home early. No dinner is anywhere in sight because I am the Homework Nazi and must check on my son every 2 minutes to make sure he is actually doing his homework. I give him a play break so he heads to the recreation room where his brother has been crying for me to help him change a Transformer back into a helicopter.

So I innocently go to the bathroom (you know this is always a mistake).

Then I hear the crash and screams.

At first I don't panic, because anyone who has children knows that this is not uncommon when a mom is in the bathroom. It is when Alex screams," Michael's bleeding!" that I jump out of the bathroom. Grab some Purell and run out to find Michael Augustus crying on the floor and his head is bleeding. He has run into a junk drawer I couldn't close because the junk would not fit back into it. Blood is on the floor, Alex is stepping in it. I look at Michael's head and he has a gouge in his forehead about one-fourth inch wide that is open and for a moment I think I can see his brain. (It was fat tissue.) Luckily, I am not faint at heart. I grab paper towels to mop up the blood. I get Michael situated laying down and have him hold an ice pack on his head. I call his father who is almost home. Michael Augustus keeps crying he just wants a Band-Aid. I keep checking on his head and wonder if he needs stitches.

Husband comes home, tries to get a hold of his dad, the surgeon. We use some medical tape to temporarily cover it. By the way, my job was to hold the skin together while my husband put the tape on. Pop Pop calls back after hearing about it; he thinks it may need some stitches. OK, so now we load the whole family into the van to go to Portland, thirty minutes away. We have to drive by McDonalds so Alex can get dinner. The rest of us decide to hold out for something better. Oh, and I forgot to mention that I haven't taken my second set of pills for the day yet and am also on the verge of a cold.

We get to his office. I get Alex set up eating french fries outside the surgery room. He finishes before anything happens so I give him some Post-its to draw pictures on. Meanwhile Michael Augustus is finally lying down. Because of the deep cut, my father-in-law says it will need a couple of stitches. Michael Augustus now has a blue paper sheet on his head because he said the light was bothering him. Luckily the paper sheet has a hole cut out for the wound. So my mother-in-law (formerly a registered nurse) is dressed in her nightgown and holding his head steady. His father has his arms, which means I am holding his legs. Pop Pop begins the stitches. In the meantime, Alex keeps wandering in to give us the drawings he has just made, completely oblivious to the hooked needle that is going into his brother's forehead. Each stitch has to be knotted about eight times. These stitches will dissolve so he won't need to get them taken out. Finally, we are done and the grandparents have promised prizes so we go outside where there is a big jar of plastic goodies. Each child gets a handful of stuff and then it is off to the car to go home and get something to eat for the rest of us.

On the way home, Michael Augustus mentions how we have been eating out too much and he is tired of all that greasy food. He suggests that maybe if we plan out dinners for the week we could eat at home more often.

HMMMMMMMMMM!

Love to all,

Kim

February 5, 2007 7:17 AM

I know I look awful. Thursday I took my shot, not many side effects. But I have been feverish once a day since. Saturday night I couldn't sleep at all. Too tired to go to church. So on Super Bowl Sunday I excused myself before the end of the bowl game and went to bed. I did sleep last night. Michael's book project was turned in today. It came out great. Yeah! His stitches have healed well. Good job, Pop Pop! Alex is less obsessed about death. And in class today, Michael held his glasses up to one eye and peered at the board. It is a start.

I am down three and a half pounds since starting this therapy. What an odd word--you would think this would be some type of therapeutic spa treatment. The good news is that I will probably look slightly better in my next picture. No promises. Although I did buy new mascara and eyeliner. The nausea hasn't been so bad today.

Love to all,

Kim

February 5, 2007 11:17 AM

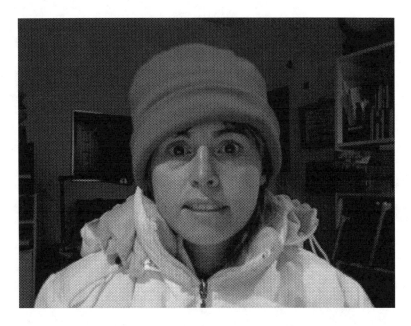

I slept for an hour or so but couldn't stay warm enough to sleep. So I took some Tylenol. Yes, this is what I wear to bed--or some variation thereof until I am warm enough. I also have a small cold, occasional sneezes. I think the most frustrating thing for me is that I am a grown-up hyperactive child and I am used to having lots of energy. Lately I have about one and a half hours of energy in the morning and then I start fading fast. I hate it. Slowing down is so not me. I see my liver doctor next week on Friday, I think. They should draw some blood then and we can see if this stuff is helping. I think if I can go back to getting regular sleep and can get rid of this cold, which is hard with my immune system being suppressed, I will feel better. I have been looking forward to doing Children's Chat and Children's Worship this Sunday. I have a great program that I made up for the kids. Whew. I just took off my hat. I am finally warming up. Once again, thank you for your prayers. I know things will work out.

Love,

Kim

February 7, 2007 7:11AM

Five weeks down and only forty-three to go: I got some sleep. Sleep is the best medicine. They should let people sleep off all illnesses. I still have a small bit of my cold, but feel much better, no feverish feelings today. So tomorrow is my next shot and also my check-in appointment with my internal medicine doctor. He is very nice.

I decided to tell the kids what is going on. I spoke with them yesterday and explained that I am not dying. I told them about my open heart surgery and losing some blood during the surgery. Then I explained about people donating blood and how some of that blood was bad blood. And now my doctors think I need to use strong medicine to zap the bad blood so it doesn't make me sick later. I also explained that the medicine was so strong that it made me tired sometimes and feverish at other times. I also explained that because I was so tired that Daddy had to bring home dinner occasionally because Mommy was too tired to make dinner. I asked them if they had questions. They had a couple. Then Michael Augustus said, "I was wondering why you were laying down on the couch so much."

Michael Augustus wore his glasses for fifteen minutes yesterday in school while I was there. I want to ask you to pray for my husband during this time. He is already swamped at work and he has had to take over laundry some days, kitchen stuff some days and boy stuff too. I know he is exhausted as well. Thanks for everything.

Love to all,
Kim

February 14, 2007 7:30PM

Good Morning All!

I am doing great. Thanks for all of the prayers. I am down 5 lbs since I started. My attitude is still positive. I will see my doctor tomorrow. Good News: Michael Augustus's book was chosen as one of three from his class to go on to the county level contest. I am very thrilled for him. Have a great day.

Kim

February 20, 2007 7:22AM

Good Evening All.

I am doing fine. I had a good appointment with my liver doctor on Friday. He said I look good and was happy that there were few side effects. I had to get blood work done to see how my body is reacting to the medicine. I have some of those results now. My white blood cell, electrolytes, liver enzymes and red blood cell count are all normal. (I have been making sure I eat beef a couple of times a week to keep my red blood cell level up. Lucky for me, I don't get the metallic taste in my mouth that some people get.) I am still waiting to hear about my hepatitis count--the level at which the disease currently exists in my system. At the beginning of the treatment it was over four million. I hope to know something within a week.

My friend, Sally Moore, sent me an email and let me know the origin of my name in Old English means 'from the meadows, seeker of truth.' I love it.

Thank you for your continued prayers.

Love,

Kim

February 22, 2007 12:45 PM

No picture this time. I can't sleep and it is not a pretty picture. Took my shot today. Eight weeks down, forty to go. It's been a difficult week. One of my sons has been getting in trouble at school for not doing what he is told to do and arguing his position with authority figures. Please understand that neither my husband nor myself condone his being rude to authority figures. But it has been a nightmare. I am so exhausted from thinking about everything. I did go to lunch with both children today at school. Please pray for both my sons as I am sure this has been difficult for them. Thank you.

Sincerely,

Kim

Side Note: I didn't know it at the time but often the children of cancer patients will start acting out when their parents are going through chemo or other treatments. I am not sure why. I would gather it is probably a mix of fear and anxiety. My doctor often refers to my treatment as chemo. But it is not as harsh as what cancer patients face. With all of the preparations I had made for my treatment and side effects, nothing prepared me for this one. However, a friend of mine helped me figure out why my child who never gets in trouble was getting in trouble. Then I was able to deal with it. I worked with both my children for several months and am happy to say they are better at helping me, helping each other and better behaved over all. It did take work and a lot of prayers. But it was worth it.

February 23, 2007 1:26:20 AM

I finally heard my blood test results. My viral load, which was over four million in January, is now at 466,000. Hurray! I'm going to try to relax. Wow, I never realized how big my teeth look. I think I can finally get a good night sleep tonight. I have had insomnia for the last two nights. Thank you for your prayers and support.

Love,

Kim

March 1, 2007 7:46 AM

Hello Everyone!

I just gave myself my shot. I am tired today. I had a lot of energy earlier in the week so I have been organizing the kids' rooms, the kitchen drawers, and my office. The counter of no return is still horrible. (For those of you who don't know, it is my kitchen counter near the phone.) One child is having a better week while the other child is going crazy trying to get my attention. No major injuries this week. One week from today my scrapbooking crew will arrive in Tennessee to go on our annual scrapbook weekend. Every year my mom and sister, Merrie, come to Tennessee to celebrate my birthday and attend a scrapbook weekend hosted by my friend Patty. It is always a great time. Just us girls staying up late laughing a lot and preserving our memories.

Hurray! I am learning to relax this week. I have also decided that I cannot control what happens at school but I can control what happens at home.

Love to all,

Kim

March 4, 2007 7:21 AM

Wow. I have just survived the worst 24 hours so far. I wasn't physically sick from the medicine. That went fine. For more than 24 hours I was suffering from depression and anxiety. It was so bad that I didn't even want to celebrate my birthday, which is tomorrow. And I always want to celebrate my birthday. I have never shied away from telling people my age. I will be 39 and that's 39 years God has given me. But yesterday and today, I have never felt so lost. I consider myself upbeat and strong, so for me not be able to control my emotions and to weep at a moment's notice was horrible.

I couldn't prevent myself from crying. I had dinner with Russ, Jill, David and Vandana last night. Every card had me in tears. I said, "I hate not being able to control my body functions." My friend David said, "Don't worry about the tears. We are just glad that you are able to control your other bodily functions." Even this morning, I had this lingering melancholy. I skipped church because I knew that anything, any thought, could start me crying and I didn't want to call attention to myself. I was angry and sad. Then Michael Augustus's fish died which gave me even more reason to cry, which I did. But after I ate lunch, I started to regain control of my emotions. It felt wonderful. And now I have the wisdom to know that God gave me a blessing. I was able to experience what people who suffer from anxiety and depression feel. I truly know their pain, the lack of concentration, the despondent feeling. I never felt suicidal. But I can truly say I have never really thoroughly understood depression until now. Please continue to pray for my children.

Love to all, May God grant you his peace

Kim

Side Note: With all that was going on, it would have been easy to lie in bed every day or phone a friend to complain about how terribly unfair things are. But I didn't. The fact is I have been blessed all my life. My blessings started with the mix-up at the hospital that prevented me from having a heart transplant when I was three months old. I didn't get into my first college pick. This was a blessing because if I hadn't gone to Emerson College I never would have competed in debate and speech and met my husband (who is one of the best husbands around). If I had been diagnosed with hepatitis C before I had children I might not have tried in the first place. I think it all comes down to God's timing in your life. You just have to trust that he has the master plan laid out for you. Of course, that doesn't mean that you should drift around not paying attention either.

Now I would be a liar if I told you that everyone I eventually told was supportive and kind. I have friends who were going to be there for me who disappeared into the woodwork. I knocked heads with school authorities about my son. At the time, I was just upset that they knew what I was going through and they still didn't give me a break. (Maybe they did in their own way. But it was hard to see that when everything was going on.) I guess it made me tougher, and a better advocate. I also worked more diligently to help my son to feel less anxious and more comfortable with school and life. Good things come out of bad things, as my mother always says.

March 14, 2007 2:59 AM

Greetings Everyone!

I am surviving. I have come to the conclusion that every week is a crazy week and there is no such thing as normal. I had a great time on my scrapbook weekend with my sister, my mom and our friend Jody. We showed Jody and Jim around Nashville and had a great time. We are ready for all of them to move to Tennessee. Alex has loved all of the extra attention. So has Michael Augustus. Please continue to pray for them.

My husband has taken off to California for a pro-am golf tournament. He really needed a break. He and his staff have been working seven days a week. As for me, I am down eight and a half pounds, have gotten a haircut, and still have some side effects. But it's not too bad right now. So it is a bit of a whirlwind week.

Love to all,

Thank you for your prayers.

Kim

Side Note: After my son started having trouble in school we began to take him to a child behavior therapist. I highly recommend this course of action for anyone whose child or children are acting up and you don't know why. She was able to figure out what was bothering him. She came up with strategies to help him and for us to work with him. She assisted us with everything from how to handle homework to lowering his anxiety. She worked with him to express his thoughts better. So now if there is something bothering him, he lets me know right away and we deal with it. We are able to openly express our feelings and we have a great relationship.

March 21, 2007 9:33 AM

No picture today. I have finished eleven weeks. Tomorrow starts the twelfth. But all of that is overshadowed tonight. A house in my subdivision is burning down. It is on the other side of the subdivision. I kept hearing sirens when I was putting the kids to bed but didn't worry too much. Michael came home after a stressful day at work and told me about the fire. When we stepped out on to the street we could see the flames into the sky. We were both amazed that it was still going. More and more fire trucks arrived. I just saw a Nashville one. I don't even know where they are putting all of the fire trucks. But it is reassuring to know how quickly and how ready everyone is there to help. I told Michael, "Makes you put things into perspective, doesn't it?" Our kids are sleeping through the entire ruckus. They are redirecting traffic away now. So all of the drive-by gawking people are turning around on our street and heading home.

Michael Augustus, while wild and rambunctious at times, has really become spiritual. He is praying of his own accord now. I witnessed him praying for God to heal him when he had been sick with a stomach virus on Sunday night. Tonight I had the stomach virus, so the kids had to play by themselves and fix themselves a healthy snack too. They did great and it was such a blessing.

Thank you for your prayers for me and for my family.

As always love,
Kim

Side Note: As I have mentioned I have always felt close to God. I think that comes from being so ill as a child and being held up spiritually by so many people in my church. I realize that not everyone is blessed with a life threatening illness as a child. But when you experience a spiritual awakening in your child, it just doesn't get better than that. For me it was such a sense of joy and relief. We have actually had conversations about how it doesn't matter when any of us die because we believe in God and Jesus, so we will see each other in heaven. I didn't fully understand this concept until a year ago. I mean I truly felt the joy from the realization that it is all going to be OK because our life on earth is just a temporary stop along the way. To have my nine-year-old understand this and accept it with confidence in God is one of my greatest accomplishments.

I think God tries to tell us things, but we are not always listening. However, on one Sunday morning in the middle of March, I woke up and felt it on my heart that I should attend our old church, St. Timothy Lutheran. I know most of you have heard of impulse purchases but not impulse worshipping. So I asked my husband to watch the kids while I went. I guess I should back up and say that I was raised Lutheran. I was baptized and confirmed Lutheran. Then, when I was in high school, the minister started going long on his sermons and that was messing up my dad's golf plans. So my father suggested we look at another church that a lot of our friends went to, the community church across town. They had a half-hour, brown bag sermon geared towards families. So we went. What I later realized is that most people went on to Sunday School. We went home. Although I must say they had a great youth group. So it actually did work out for the best.

Getting back to my original explanation . . . when I first moved to Tennessee we went regularly to St. Timothy for several years and even played on their softball team. But then there came a time when we started running late to church every week. Sometimes, if we were really late, we didn't even go. So my husband suggested that we try out a new church closer to home. He suggested the cute, historic church behind the Sonic. I told him you couldn't pick a church because it is cute. But I said I would be willing to try it one Sunday. So we did. And you will never guess what happened. They brought me a loaf of homemade bread. Oh, how I love good bread. So I was willing to go again. Well, pretty soon we had people our age greeting us and making us feel welcome. We felt so welcome that when our first son was born, we joined the Connell United Methodist Church. And that was that! I thought.

Well, anyone who takes the opportunity to get involved in a church of any kind is going to get his or her feelings hurt now and then. It just happens. Some people turn it into a turf war, some just leave and some take a break every now and then. I had taken a couple of breaks over the years but had always come back to Connell. Then that Sunday, even though I had the support of my whole Sunday School class, I just felt it in my heart that I should attend service at St. Timothy that morning. As I sat there in the pew, I asked God to let me know if this was where I was supposed to be. By the time the service was over, I felt as though I had come home. I think that is how you are supposed to feel at church, no matter what your religion. The irony is that the Lutheran service is fifteen minutes longer than the Methodist one. I guess I am making up for all that time we missed out on when I was a teenager. Just kidding. I am thankful to say that I have friends at both churches.

March 26, 2007 9:36:09 PM

I am having an 80s hair kind of day. I hope you are all well. So here is the update. I feel ok. This week's side effects have been mostly fatigue and pain in my bones. I can deal with it. I am down ten pounds and have tried to start slowing my weight loss by eating pop tarts and ice cream.

With thirty-six more shots to go, I was concerned I may be losing weight too fast. The benefits are I can now wear my smaller clothes and I look better on the outside. And of course to look good is to feel good . . .

My children are beginning to relax more. My latest blood work showed that my cholesterol, white blood cell count and red blood cell count were in normal range. Next month I will have my next viral load count done. Oooh, can't wait.

Love to all,

Thank you for your continued prayers.

Love,

Kim

PS. I drew that picture behind my head, in case you didn't know.

Date: April 7, 2007 4:55:53 AM

Hello Everyone!

My ongoing antiviral therapy is no worse, and sometimes better. I will probably have my blood work run this week. As soon as I know the new viral count, I will of course let you know. It probably will take a week. The boys are getting along. Their behavior has been good. We are continuing to work on manners.

Happy Easter to all of you!

Love,

Kim

THEN ALONG CAME THE TENNESSEE COUSINS

In March when I realized my kids were really stressed out from homework and our chaotic lifestyle, I decided to remedy the situation with more play dates. Back in February, I had offered to pick up Meri Allen, a girl we knew from church, and bring her home. Her mom had to pick up four kids at different times and at three different places. Because of our crazy schedule, I could only pick her up on one day a week. Well, I asked her one day if she would like to come over and play with the boys after school one day. She said sure. I okayed it with her mom. Well, after a big snack and a crazy game of Uno, we started making it a regular homework study group/play date.

Finally it occurred to me that my friend's husband worked late some nights and so did mine. I called her up and invited her and the kids over for a silly supper. We had pizza and root beer and ice cream treats for dessert. The kids played Uno. But mostly, the six kids ranging in age from four to eight had a fantastic time playing in our backyard in the dirt. By the end of the night, they were all covered in dirt with huge smiles on their faces. I told Michael Augustus that I had never met anyone who liked dirt as much as he did until that night.

It made me remember all of the good times with my cousins I had growing up. My in-laws are the only family we have in Tennessee, so an idea started to form. So a week or two later, I asked my friend if they had cousins in Tennessee. She said, "No." I said, "Well, neither do we. Why don't we adopt you as our Tennessee cousins!"

So we have treated each other like family ever since. It has been a huge blessing to my kids and me. While I have other family and the kids have lots of other cousins, we only get to see them once a year or once every couple of years. It is truly a treat to be Wild and Crazy Aunt Kim.

April 12, 2007 10:34 PM

I am sitting here laughing out loud. This was the fifth picture I took. The earlier four pictures didn't look right. My left eye appeared bigger than my right. After the four times, I realized I hadn't put mascara on my other eye. I just took shot number fifteen yesterday. I am doing well. My general blood work came back normal. I will get my viral count next week sometime. Things are calming down at my house as we focus on having play dates, sit down meals and finishing our homework in a relaxed manner. Life is good. God is great. And you all are wonderful. Thank you for your prayers, they have been working.

Love,

Kim

April 17, 2007 10:08 PM

Hi Everyone,

Yesterday, I found out that the test that had been run was the wrong one. It just said my viral count was greater than 7500. So I will have to have my blood drawn again this Friday and then wait another ten days to find out.

Ugh! Oh well. I am over it today. I have finally reached my goal. I am the Kool Aid mom. I had our Tennessee Cousins over yesterday and made Kool Aid and whipped up eight grilled cheese sandwiches on my new grill pan. It is cool. It is a big rectangle pan that fits over two burners. I made all of the sandwiches at once. Amazing! The kids had a great time with their cousins and we even went to watch Ana Karlin at soccer practice. I have to go for now. Have a great week.

Love,

Kim

April 19, 2007 10:16:37 PM

Hello again. I just got back from my liver doctor. I have mixed news but overall good. My red blood cell stuff is a bit lower. If it gets too low I will become tired more quickly. He said that is because of the medicine. He will keep a watch on it. However, he did notice that one of the things tested seems to be decreasing, which he seemed to think meant the inflammation in my liver was decreasing. So that is the happier part. Overall, he thinks I am doing well. I had my blood test re-run this morning so I probably won't know my viral count for a week and a half. Otherwise life is good. Thank you for the continued prayers.

Love to All,

Kim

May 2, 2007 8:15 AM

Hello Everyone,

I finally have the latest results of my viral count. Previously my count had come down to 450,000. My most recent test has the count at 59,800. So that's progress. Some people are able to rid the virus within a couple of months. But I have never been like most people, so I will wait. Plus, the virus has been happily living in my liver for over thirty years. So I could see why it might have a hard time leaving. Yes, I did put on lipstick just for you all. Doesn't everyone wear lipstick to bed? Life is good. Michael is doing well in school with straight A's. Neither one of my sons has gotten in trouble in a long time. I have loved helping out in Spanish class and I have even learned a little. Alex is getting excited about his birthday party on Monday. We invited his class after school to Circus World. Alex is the king for his party and he has invited his friends to help him defeat the enormous goofy dragon that is attacking his castle. It should be fun.

I hear Alex crying. Gotta go.

Love to all of you,

Kim

May 16, 2007 6:59 AM

Wow. I can't believe it. Tomorrow starts the 20th week. Almost halfway through and I have so much to report. First of all, thank you to all of you who have been praying for me. My family is at peace. I love helping out in school. Maybe I will get a teacher certification someday. Secondly, you are all invited to my home on Saturday, June 16th at 6:30 PM for my "Life Is Sweet Party." We will have cheese, fruit, desserts and beverages to celebrate the halfway mark in my treatment. As far as treatment goes, I am still holding up well. I have noticed that I am shedding a bit more hair lately. But not to worry, I have a lot of hair and I usually shed. (I must have been a puppy in a former life. That would explain the big brown eyes.) Alex celebrated his 6th birthday with a dragon cake made by me. I will send the picture later. I have been working like crazy to finish the kindergarten scrapbooks. And today, I spoke to Alex's class about my former career as an investment broker. I finished with Financial Advice for Kindergarteners.

Love Always,

Kim

May 20, 2007 10:20PM

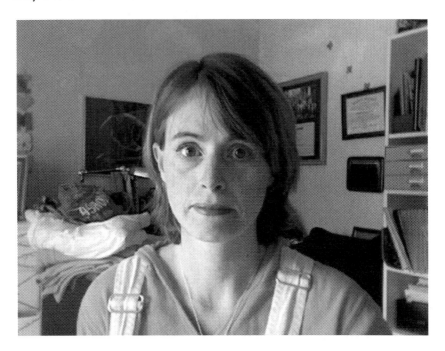

Hello All,

Last week I had an intestinal virus, which left me by Saturday. I was tired, but I thought I was otherwise fine. For some reason, I decided to take the kids back to Connell Church this weekend. I am glad I did. By the time we got from the car to the front of the church, my heart was pounding strongly. After we got situated in the balcony, I started feeling flushes of heat through my chest and arms. If you have ever had a CT scan, it felt like it does when they inject the dye. This happened several times. I didn't know what was happening and I just prayed for God to help me. Along came my friend Lori Sutton (a former nurse) up to the balcony to sit with her daughter. So I moved next to her and told her my symptoms and also about my hep-C and the antiviral therapy. She said it sounded like dehydration. The flushes of heat stopped about twenty minutes later.

I decided to go straight home after the service while I was feeling up to it. My husband was at a golf match and someone else had driven. My father-in-law, the doctor, arrived around 12:30. I told him what was happening and had him listen to my heart, which was skipping about every twentieth beat. He felt that I had run too low on potassium and magnesium from all of the dehydration. So he ran to the store for me and got me magnesium tablets, bananas and Pedialyte to help hydrate me. He also watched the kids until my husband got home. Then while my husband took the kids to a birthday party, Pop Pop stayed with me. He checked my heart rate again and said it was beating fine. I still feel weak. So I am trying to conserve energy. Alex graduates from kindergarten tomorrow night. So I want to be up for that.

Love,

Kim

Side Note: I hope to never go through that again. I have had a heart condition all my life. I have not been on meds for my condition for as long as I can remember. So I am not used to having any problems with my heart except if I run too much. Then I get red in the face and really tired. I believe that God answered my prayer sending Lori. She helped to calm me down. One of the things that I have relied on is my ability to use mind over matter. If I can find a logical explanation for something, I don't worry about it as much. My mind accepts it for fact and I simply go on. This technique has worked for me all my life. I now know that God tells us not to be anxious in Philippians 4:6-7.

"Do not be anxious about anything, but in everything, by prayer and petition, with thanksgiving, present your requests to God. And the peace of God will guard your hearts and minds in Christ Jesus."

Of course the mind over matter works the opposite way too. If I can come up with something dreadful as an explanation for a pain or discomfort, my mind will also accept it as possible fact. So that makes me a bit of a hypochondriac. My husband is used to my hypochondriac ways. For instance in the past, if I got a headache, I would tell my husband how I never get headaches so it was probably something serious. Could it be a tumor? My husband used to roll his eyes. Now if I mention that my head hurts, he cuts me off and says, "Must be a tumor."

May 25, 2007 7:35:09 PM

Just wanted to send a little note--to let you know that I am back to being hydrated and have not had any more problems since last Monday. This week's symptoms are nausea and joint aches. The boys are out of school. We had a great last week of school. Hope all of you are well.

Love,

Kim

June 4, 2007 6:16:46 PM

Hello All,

I am getting ready for day two of Vacation Bible School at St. Timothy's. I am the photographer. I am trying to fight off a bit of melancholy. My liver specialist wrote me an update based on my last viral count. He had expected the viral count to drop much more than it has. He even mentioned considering lengthening the treatment. I am starting to wake up with some hair on my pillow as my hair is beginning to thin. Otherwise I am good. I have decided to take extra vitamins to help with my hair. Once again, God gave me an enormous amount of hair, so it will be awhile before the thinning is noticeable. I have found over the past couple of months that it has been good for me to distract myself by helping others. Well, I'm off to VBS.

Love,

Kim

Side Note: I had a wonderful "Life Is Sweet Party" with 8 friends. We ate and played music. I had found a blue guitar, a bongo drum and a ukulele at a garage sale for only $60. I have no musical talent. But they looked beautiful and I figured if I had a guest over who knew how to play, I would be set. So at my party we jammed. I wailed on that bongo drum wearing a plaid party dress and curled up hair. It was just what I needed to keep me going.

My husband joined me for my next visit to Dr. Mike. Dr. Mike told me in person that the virus was not leaving as fast as he would have liked. Usually they want a patient to get to zero and then stay on the treatment for an additional six months to get rid of any residual cells of the disease. I was five and a half months in and I still wasn't to zero. This was depressing news. My husband asked if there was something stronger that I could take to get rid of it. I almost punched him. Looking back, he just wanted me to have a successful treatment. But at the time the thought of making the side effects worse was inconceivable. The doctor gave me three options. I could continue on the course that I was on, I could up the dosage of what I was on (which was getting me close to being anemic), or I could switch to the non-pegylated interferon and give myself daily shots instead of weekly ones. I chose to continue on for as long as I could stand it.

I left the office quite dejected. So there were no updates for a while. I had my blood drawn again and awaited the results again. At least I have good veins, so it was always easy to get my blood drawn. My poor mother-in-law, every time they draw her blood, she looks like she got mugged in an alley. She also has the uncanny ability to attract nursing students who have no idea what they are doing. No offense is intended to those nursing students who do know what they are doing. Then finally I broke my silence:

Tuesday, July 17, 2007 6:56 AM

Hello Everyone:

Sorry I have not given you an update in awhile. As you all know, I started antiviral therapy on January 4 of this year with a viral count of 4,555,000. As of July 6th it is down to 105. If I completely clear the virus from my bloodstream I will be one of the 50 percent of those on this treatment who have succeeded. It has come at a bit of a cost. I am now anemic, which causes extreme fatigue, heart problems and I have been losing more hair since June. You still can't tell because God blessed me with a whole lot of hair. They want to extend my treatment by thirty-six weeks once I reach zero to get rid of whatever may remain in the tissues of my body. They will soon be giving me a medicine for the anemia.

I have decided to continue the medicine until I get to zero and then decide a week at a time how long I will continue. I have learned many things along this road. God has blessed me with experiences that I might not have experienced otherwise. Please pray that God would heal what the medicines could not.

Thank you for your prayers.

Love to all,

Kim

July 20, 2007 9:37 AM

Howdy Folks!

As you can see I still have lots of hair. As many of you have observed, since I have started this process, I have had a lot of challenges along the way. Being optimistic and upbeat, I have tried to find the blessing in each circumstance. That is how Dr. Ray, my internal medicine doctor (the one I trust the most), helped me come up with my name. When life gives you lemons, make lemonade. And I am the Queen of Lemonade, although even I have fallen from my throne recently and have been the best pity party planner you have ever met. Of course, I would have invited you all to attend my very special pity parties, but they were parties for one. I am starting to stop obsessing over my hair loss, even though I still find my hair in my food every day.

I just took the new medicine--they prescribed Procrit--which it turns out is another injection with giant needles, and the side effects are aches, pains, swelling and fevers. Whoo Hoo! What fun! I practically gave myself a puncture wound when I self-injected on Wednesday night. Oh, and did I mention the bubbles? For those of you who have never had to inject yourself using a needle, you must get the bubbles out of the needle before injecting. Well the new medicine looked as though it had been mixed with champagne. I finally broke into a second vial to get enough medicine without bubbles.

Ah and now the good news . . . I have met my drug deductible for the year. Lately, I need to rest a lot, so I have had to ask the boys to do more for me. They have been great. Also, in the middle of my onslaught of pity parties, a couple of weeks ago, I decided to make a list of crimes and punishments for the kids, which has been hanging from the refrigerator. I am now taking the Giuliani approach to parenting: Take them off the street on the first offense and make them do some time for their crime. It is working better than anything I have tried. In fact, my children have gone from some of the worst behaving children that I have ever met to some of the best. I was even at Burger King on Wednesday and a man complimented me on how I was doing a great job with my kids. He had noticed them opening the door for me and taking turns to order their own food. I have missed our mail chats. I hope you are all well.

I guess what I am trying to say is . . . The Queen has returned to make more lemonade.

Love,

Kim

Side Note: I was getting more tired each week. I would set myself up on the couch and spend more time than I care to remember watching Power Rangers with the boys because I didn't have the energy to do much else. Occasionally, I would save up my energy and take the boys for a play date at the pool. Then I would smile, wave good-bye and flop back down on the couch. Meals were simple. Usually something I could throw on a pan and put in the oven for the kids. My husband was able to fend for himself most of the time. He also brought home dinner a couple of times a week.

July 27, 2007 5:34 PM "The Sweetest Lemonade of All Is Family."

Well, I have had the sweetest lemonade of all. The medicine I complained about last week seems to be kicking in. I actually had a full day of energy. I kept waiting to drop, but I didn't yesterday. Today I was ready to nap at 1:30 PM, but my mom and Frank are here, so I could nap. Now we are on our way to dinner. The kids are behaving great. They are such a pleasure. Oh, the funny Alex story of the month took place this week, while I was visiting my cousin Carrie in Buffalo, New York. My younger cousin Greg was there, who is 23 and a former high school wrestler. So he let the kids wrestle him and pound on him for the whole trip. When we were packed in the car ready to go to the airport, my cousin Greg walked us out and said good-bye to Alex who was already in the car. He told Alex, "You can give me one more punch." So Alex did. He punched him in the head. Be careful what you ask for or you just might get it. Thank you, friends and family, for your continued support and prayers.

Love always,

Kim

August 2, 2007 11:03 AM

Hey Everyone:

Me again. Just spoke with Dr. Mike (my liver doctor). Somehow my test that usually takes a week took only two days. He said my viral count had gone up to 450 something. So he is concluding that the virus has become resistant to the medication. I am down to two options--stopping all of the medicine or taking daily injections of something similar. After talking with Dr. Mike at length, he thought and I agreed that I should stop the medicine. He feels that there are new medicines coming out in a few years, after they go through clinical trials; they might work better for me. I could choose the daily injections, but since it is just a slightly different version of what I am already taking, it may also be resistant or not work too well. I will have my blood tested in two weeks and see if I need to continue on the Procrit. So the bad news is I am not completely rid of the virus. But the good news is that I have brought the numbers down to a very low amount. And I can stop taking the medication that makes my hair fall out and makes me feel so terrible. I can also donate my unused medicine to their office so that when they have a patient who can't afford it, they can give them some of mine.

As many of you recall, I didn't look sick or feel sick before I started this treatment, so I will hopefully go back to the normal me. I do not fear my future. God is with me and has always been with me. I know he has a plan for me. By the way, if you haven't seen Evan Almighty yet, go see that movie. It is light and entertaining. There is a great dialogue in the movie when Evan turns to God and tells him that he is ruining all of his plans, and God just laughs and laughs until Evan realizes how ridiculous he sounds.

Thank you for all of your prayers and support. If something changes I will keep you posted.

And now for the Alex story of the week: My mom and Frank came to visit us and they are Catholic, so we attended the local Catholic church. We forgot to bring something for the kids to do quietly in the pew. So I had let Alex sit on my lap a couple of times. My mom and Frank went up to receive communion. Alex was sitting on my lap facing me when suddenly he said, "Mom, the other day I saw a commercial on the television and if you want to get rid of the fur on your face, you can order this thing and it takes it right off. Really!" I was dying laughing. I used to have a mole on my chin. I had the mole removed several years ago but the hair still grows out where the mole once was. I guess I better get out the scissors.

I hope you all realize that I am very happy to stop this medicine and am looking forward to many things like having energy for a full day, being able to exercise, letting Alex play with my hair again, being able to concentrate long enough to play chess with Michael Augustus, and being able to travel and explore without feeling completely wiped out.

Love,

Kim

Side Note: Two weeks before, I had prayed to God that if the treatment was not going to work to please let me know somehow. I had met with Dr. Ray and told him that I had wanted to give up the treatment. It was getting too tough. I felt terrible. I was basically asking his permission to quit. Well, he surprised me when he told me that every cancer patient gets to a point when they want to quit treatment too. But he said, "If you quit now and your numbers go up or you get worse . . . you will always wonder if. What would have happened if I had stayed with it?" I knew he was right. I just didn't want to hear it. So I did stay with it, and what do you know, my viral count went up and I got off the antiviral therapy. So it was worth waiting. I think it's important to surround yourself with good influence people when you need advice. You will usually hear what you need to, not what you want to.

August 8, 2007 6:29 A.M

Hello,

My head does not feel right today so that is why it is tipping over in the picture. The day after I stopped using the medicines, I have been hit with a terrible series of headaches, the kind you have from a hangover. When I bend down to pick something up and come back up it feels as though something hits me in the head every time. I had been having trouble sleeping but finally got a full night last night. I spoke with the nurse in charge of my treatment yesterday and she said insomnia and headaches usually don't happen from coming off the medicine.

So I think I will call Dr. Fuller today. I know I am such a baby, but I rarely have headaches. Yesterday, Michael Augustus stopped me from buying Swiss Rolls in the snack aisle at Target. I was about to give in and grab a box of comfort food. I grabbed the box and Michael Augustus said, "No, Mommy. Don't get those. Don't you remember last time we got them. They tasted good but they didn't fill us up." He took a box and started to read 270 calories and 12 grams of fat. I put them back and told Michael, "Thank you." I then decided to get Peanut Butter

Captain Crunch instead--much healthier you know, only 110 calories, 2.5 grams of fat and lots of sprayed on vitamins. On a positive note, the boys' behavior continues to amaze me in a good way. I think they are going to have a great year. My energy level is returning. It is only my head that is slowing me down now. I know--complain, complain, complain. I hope you are all well.

Love,

Kim

August 12, 2007 8:19 PM

Hello Everyone.

What a week it has been! I had a headache for eight days straight and bouts of insomnia. I was able to help the pain with various over the counter medicines, but it wouldn't go away. I finally called my father-in-law, Dr. Ponce, and my friend, Dr. Hunt. They both felt that part of the headache could have been caused from going off the medicine. I left a message for my liver doctor which he apparently never received. So I saw my father-in-law at dinner on Thursday night and he suggested that it might be the anemia again. He said to come by the office and they could test for it in the morning. So on Friday morning, I packed up the boys and we headed to Portland. My father-in-law was right. My count had gone down to 9.5, which means I was very anemic.

I had already scheduled a haircut for myself so I headed to that next. By the time I arrived, I was extremely pale and very weak. I told my hairdresser, Cheryl, that I hadn't slept well and had a headache. She suggested she wash my hair and massage my head so I would feel better. After she washed my hair she leaned into me and said, "OK, what's going on . . . your hair is falling out . . . I have already cleared the drain out twice?" So I told her an abbreviated version of what I have been through. We have always joked about me having enough hair for two people. She thinks I have lost half of mine--because she remembers how thick it was, So I told her, "Thank goodness God gave me a lot of hair." Well, I went home with wet hair, afraid to blow dry any more away. I took my shot with the giant needle. Of course the small needle would not fit on the giant needle. I called Anna at my liver doctor's office and left her a message that I would need more Procrit. She called me back and when she heard my numbers, she said, "So are you just crawling around?" At least the Procrit worked. I only had to take one dose of pain medicine on Saturday and none today. It has made me think, though, how did my red blood cell numbers drop three points in ten days? I am beginning to wonder if my test results were accurate. So to ease my mind I am going to ask for them to be redone.

Well, I made it to church today. I didn't stand a lot but I made it and registered the kids for Sunday School. On Saturday we took the kids to Wave Country--a city owned water park. The kids had a blast and it was fun doing something as a family again. I even went down a couple of water slides. Oh you should have seen me, getting into my luge stance hurtling down the watery tubes. It was like watching the Olympics. Well, not really, but it was fun.

I think the biggest lesson I have learned from this experience is to stop putting off things for when you have time. There will never be time. If something is important you have to make it a priority. I shall step off my soapbox now.

And now a picturesque description of Alex at Wave Country: So Alex, who is thirty-six inches tall and only forty-one pounds big, grabs a hold of a clear inner tube and heads for deeper water as the waves begin in the pool. I am walking/running through the water to catch up to him. I swim after him and grab a hold of the tube that he is in. I am now above my head in wave filled water and Alex decides to abandon the tube so he can head for the ladder. He winds up holding on to the ladder, his little legs swinging back and forth as the waves knock him into the wall. People near the ladder are trying to help him get up the ladder. He finally makes it up the ladder, walks to the edge of the pool and jumps in again. And that's why we call him Alexander Danger Ponce.

I hope all is well and that you are all healthy, and if not healthy, having a good week anyway.

Love,

Kim

August 17, 2007 7:49 PM

Your love of life will carry you through any circumstance. At least that's what my fortune cookie said tonight. I had to smile when I got that fortune. I am feeling much better. The prayers are working. I just took my weekly shot of Procrit tonight.

The last couple of days have been so much better. I volunteered at the boys' school Monday through Thursday in various classes. I will admit that on Monday and Tuesday, I felt shaky a couple of times. I know what you're thinking; you're looking at this picture and saying she really shouldn't go out without lipstick or that I shouldn't volunteer so much until I'm better. But helping others is so rewarding and helps me to curb my desire to hold pity parties. I am feeling so much stronger now; instead of wanting to have pity parties I have begun to feel indignant at times. So I will have to watch that. Don't worry, I haven't told anyone off yet. Well, the boys had their first week at school. It went well. Michael likes his teacher. Alex is another story. I started good habits again this week. I walked twenty minutes and then thirty minutes two days later and then forty minutes this morning. I also made healthier food choices this week. Not on every meal, just here and there. Hey, it is a start. I am up to page five in my book. And I even fluffed up my hair a bit today.

OK, now for Alex and his new teacher. On Tuesday, he saw me at lunch and looked sad. I asked, "Alex, what is the matter?" He said he got in trouble. I asked how and Alex said," Well, Nicholas and I were talking and Mrs. Pinson heard us. I think she has ears in the back of her head. And then I had to pull a warning card. So now I think I might lose time on the playground. I want to quit school!" I assured him that it was against the law to quit school so he would have to tough it out. Later, at pickup, he got in the car and was smiling. He said, "Mom, do you know what the best part of getting the warning card was?" "No," I replied. "The best part was that it was too hot to go on the playground today! So I didn't lose any time. Sweet!" (At this point he throws his arms up in the air and says, "Everybody Dance Now," and he starts singing and dancing.)

Thank you for your continued prayers and support.

Love,

Kim

August 21, 2007 12:07PM

OK, so I took my Procrit on Friday. On Sunday, I noticed a rash around my mouth. (I had noticed one a couple of weeks ago.) On a hunch, I decided to look up what the side effects for Procrit were on the Internet. I Googled and found a list of class action lawsuits that are against the makers of Procrit and like substances. Apparently, there have been people who have been experiencing seizures, heart attacks and other scary stuff. Procrit is also made with a substance from donated blood. Also not what I wanted to hear considering that is how this all started in the first place. Notice, today is Tuesday and I am appearing happy-ish. I decided not to email you at once and rant and rave.

I did, however, meet with Dr. Ray, my voice of reason (Internal Medicine). I let him know everything that went on since last month. And I thanked him for convincing me not to quit treatment last month. He was right--I would have felt horrible if I had quit and then had gotten my viral count showing a raised number. I asked him how I could get off of the Procrit. He said that as long as the medicines were still in my system, my kidneys were probably going to have a hard time. You never know, my kidneys could kick in sooner. I remember that the medicine could last as long as 6 months in your system. So I will have my blood tested often to see when my blood levels are normal and start decreasing it from there with a doctor's permission. I also had a killer headache Sunday night and Monday morning, which by the way are also side effects. Am I the only one who thinks this is crazy? I think my body has aged about five years going through this process but I have gained ten years of knowledge and wisdom.

Love,

Kim

August 25, 2007 10:10 AM

Hello!

I have had more headaches this week. When I described how it felt to friends, they said it sounded like a migraine. So I guess I am having mini-migraines. Wow! I don't know how people survive having these regularly. I mean how could they hold down a job? I woke up from the pain of one at 4:00 AM the day before and last night the medicines wore off as I finally fell asleep around 1:00 AM So needless to say, I haven't gotten much sleep and it has been a painful night. My husband gave up his early morning bicycle ride this morning so I could sleep in. These migraines are a side effect of the Procrit. At least the rash around my mouth is starting to go away. I had my blood tested on Wednesday and all my red blood cell counts are up. So the liver doctor's nurse said I could stop taking Procrit. But my father-in-law said I really should test in two weeks to get a more accurate count. So I will remain optimistic but cautious about my numbers. I meet with my cardiologist this week and my liver specialist. As I made the bed this morning, my pillow was covered with hair. I guess it was all of that tossing and turning last night. You know, I was thinking Barbie doesn't have that much hair on her head either and it hasn't hurt her any. So I will be fine. On a positive note, I had started to gain weight in the beginning of August and now I am back down. (I mean I should get some benefit out of this eight-month makeover!)

On the home front, the boys finished up their second week of school. Alex has only pulled one more warning card. Once again it was too hot for recess. So when we got into Ritter's, a local ice cream place, he clasped his hands together and said, "Dear God, thank you for making today so hot. Amen."

OK guys, that is all the concentration I have.

Have a great day! And I hope you all have a migraine free year. I guess the blessing in this is that now I truly know what it is like for people who have migraines.

Love,

Kim

August 29, 2007 4:50 PM

Hello All,

No headaches since Saturday. Yeah! Good news from my cardiologist today. He said my heart sounds great and that my echocardiogram from a couple of weeks ago looked good too. The kids are still doing well in school. And today I was the substitute art teacher for the afternoon. I survived. I have decided the fifth graders were the easiest to work with. So after I cleaned up the art room, I left school with the boys. I mentioned that the school would pay me for being a substitute. Alex said, "Sweet!" They wanted to know how much money I had made. I said, "Well, a substitute makes $50 for a whole day, and I only worked a half day, so that is $25. Of course after taxes it is probably only $10. So that means we can go to Ritter's twice." Alex said, "Wow, we get to go twice! Sweet!"

I see my liver doctor on Friday to put together a plan of action. Can you believe one year ago this week, I had my biopsy, found out my prognosis and later decided to schedule antiviral therapy?

I realized today that if my son hadn't fallen behind in Spanish, I wouldn't have volunteered in his Spanish class, and then I wouldn't have watched how the children learned and how teachers taught, and then I never would have come up with my Spanish learning blocks to help children learn how to put together grammatical sentences in Spanish (which I plan to market once I figure out how to do that.) So good things do come out of bad things if you are willing to be patient and look for the positive.

Thank you for your prayers. Have a fabulous day and a wonderful week.

Love,

The Queen of Lemonade

September 1, 2007 11:11 AM

Hello Everyone,

Well, here I am one year later after that first biopsy. I met with Dr. Mike yesterday. He told me, "Well, we tried and it didn't work." (OK, who writes his material? It could use a little work.) Antiviral therapy is only successful in 40-50 percent of the people who try it. But it was still kind of shocking to hear him say it that way. He is actually a nice guy. He explained that without the drugs in my system my viral count would probably go up. He would no longer monitor my viral count because I was not on any medicine to lower it. I will have my regular blood panel run every six months, meet with him once a year and have a biopsy every three to five years (because it was so much fun the first time) to see if there is further damage to my liver. He also said that if a trial for a new medicine comes up that he thinks would work for me, he would call me sooner. I handed over my leftover medicine so that someone else could use it and left for lunch.

The other night when I mentioned it was dessert time to the kids, Michael Augustus said, "Dessert, we don't really need that. It isn't very healthy." So I said he was right. Then I told them that this was the last time to eat before bed. Alex piped up and said, "Mom, can we please have something from the healthy snack basket instead?" "Sure," I replied. At least I am raising two healthy boys who can take care of me when I am older.

So the good news is I am not dying yet. The bad news is I am back to where I started a year ago. Well, sort of. I mean my liver situation is probably the same. But I have grown. I have been given the gift of empathy. I have walked in the shoes of those suffering from depression, migraine headaches, fatigue, hair loss, chemo side effects, insomnia, and those who suffer anxiety and other medical and stress related ailments. I have had to chase pills under the table at restaurants or dig them out of the bottom of my purse because the pill box came open, and at $40 a pop, they weren't getting left behind. But I have also enjoyed getting to know different people who have come into my life. I have extended my family in Tennessee. I have marveled at how exciting it is to watch kids learn, especially when they finally understand a concept. So am I cured of the virus? No. Am I cured of apathy, wasting time, laziness and being fearful of what others think? I think I am.

Back in July, when things had gotten really bad, I prayed to God that if the medicines weren't going to heal me to please let me know somehow. Then my numbers went down and then up. So I feel I got my answer. I am feeling so much better physically now that I have been off the antiviral therapy for four weeks and the Procrit for two weeks. I only had one migraine this week. Today as I brushed my hair and watched it come out, I realized God must have given me three times the normal amount of hair. I am so lucky. There are so many of you who encouraged me along the way, lifted me up when I was down, led by example, openly prayed for me in your responses and prayed for me on your own. Thank you for supporting me through this eight-month roller coaster ride. With God's help, my experience will help others.

Love to all,

Kim

P.S. I turn 40 in March and I plan to have a drink. Goodness knows I have felt like having one since starting this craziness. I won't overdo it, I promise. And if you ask my children they will tell you, I always keep my promises.

Part 3

—◦◦◦—

Recipes for a Joyful Life

"I want us to help each other with the faith we have. Your faith will help me, and my faith will help you." Romans 1:12 NCV

Chapter 4

Joy Is Part of God's Plan

I am an optimist. I think sometimes optimists get a bad name. But I believe that God is the eternal optimist. Think about it. When everyone else gives up on you he is still there waiting, just hoping, that you will turn to him and receive his love and all he has to give. You and I know that we are not perfect. We are far from it. There was only one perfect person to walk the earth and that was Jesus. Yet God loves us anyway.

God has faith in us. He continues to believe that we will do good, to do right, to help and love others. He believes in us, he trusts us to do the right thing. I feel in so many ways we are his teenagers. We have our independence, we know what we are supposed to do, we know the rules, we know what is expected and yet . . . .Hmmm, I think we start out doing the right stuff, but just like teenagers we find ourselves doing what we want, not what our parents wants us to do. I don't know about you but when I do what God wants me to do I feel this unbelievable joy inside: joy that is so wonderful that I feel like I am smiling on the inside; joy that bubbles up inside me and pours out smiles on the outside. It goes up to my eyes and shines through as sparkles.

Joy is part of God's plan. Do you know that we are predisposed to feel joy? We have actually been built to be joyful. God wants all of us to realize and experience joy, not just a chosen few. Our bodies are actually built to react differently to good thoughts and bad thoughts. According to Dr. Daniel Amen, author of Change Your Brain, Change Your Life, your brain releases chemicals when you think thoughts. Through Spect scans and research, he has been able to determine that when you think positive thoughts, your brain releases chemicals that calm your heart and soothe your insides. When you have negative/anxious thoughts, your brain releases chemicals that make your heart race, your muscles tense and truly make you feel uncomfortable in your own skin. Have you ever been having a good time and suddenly noticed someone who has been unkind to you or your family. You stop smiling, your body becomes tense, and you may even clench your fists.

God wants us to feel good about each other and ourselves. In the book of Philippians chapter 4, verses 6-7, we are told, "Do not be anxious about anything, but in everything, by prayer and petition, with thanksgiving, present your requests to God. And the peace of God will guard your hearts and your minds in Christ Jesus." You may be thinking it can't be that easy. I have to suffer first. I have to do one hundred items on the "how to get to heaven list". People don't often believe that there is an easier way.

For example, let me tell you a little story. Many years ago the makers of an antibiotic cream created a non-stinging cream. They were very excited about this new product. But just to be sure they decided to test market it. After having participants test the cream, they were surprised by the reactions. Most of the participants said they would not buy the cream because they didn't think it worked. They equated the stinging with the effectiveness of the cream. So the company went back to the lab and added a tiny bit of alcohol to the mix and put their product on the market which became an instant success. Unbelievable!

Why do we find it so hard to have a relationship with God? Do we think we will be giving up something? Do we think we will have to suffer first or feel stinging before we feel relief? I think God wants us not only to experience joy, but he also wants us to spread that joy to others. Just to be clear, I am not advocating that we just try to make people happy on a superficial level by giving them things or telling them they are wonderful. That will get you a happy moment here or there but that is not what joy is about. That will win you some superficial friends. But I am talking about going deeper. You only have to look at Dale Carnegie's book, How to win friends and influence people to see examples of using positive thoughts, compliments, listening and being respectful of others to gain success. Mr. Carnegie is right about the way we should treat others with respect and take the time to listen to what others are saying. The Bible says in Mathew 7:12 "So in everything, do to others what you would have them do to you, for this sums up the Law and the Prophets." So we share our joy and spread it to others by first showing each other respect, taking the time to listen and acknowledging each other.

For me, I feel that God put it on my heart to share my story of what I went through when I was battling a potentially fatal disease. So I am sharing what I learned from him during that time.

I started attending a women's Bible study and began to take the time to get to know other people in the group a little bit better. I shared small bits and pieces. Then one day I brought a couple of copies of my unpublished book, and when someone asked me about my opinion, I said I can tell you the short answer or you can read my whole story. It surprised everyone. But I had two copies and two people picked them up. These copies have been passed around from person to person in my group and around the church. I have received thank yous, hugs and smiles like you wouldn't believe just from sharing. The irony is that when I started my treatments, very few people knew what I was going through. With each person I eventually told, my burden grew lighter. God wants us to share the good and the bad with each other and him. He already knows what is in our hearts. He can help us to grow from the hard experiences of our life and make better experiences. I know that for a fact.

I realize that not everyone has been blessed by having a childhood illness or wants to write a book to share their good news. But you can experience joy by reaching out to others in different ways. You can share your experiences or just give a helping hand. I found that helping others was not only rewarding but a fabulous distraction from the blahs of going through treatment. I would ask you each to find some way to help out another person even if it is only once a week. There is a lot of joy that comes from helping others. The more I become involved in helping others the better I feel.

I know God loves me. I know he loves all of you. But until recently, I didn't understand that God can show his love through the people we surround ourselves with. When I began to share my story at St. Timothy

Lutheran Church, I was overwhelmed with the love and kindness that people showed me. I have a much deeper bond with many of the people there now. I feel God's love from the people all around me. I want everyone to feel that kind of love. You know why because it just makes you want to spread that love around.

A Quick Prayer

Dear God, Heavenly Father,

We are just your teenagers here on earth. Please forgive us. We know right from wrong and yet we tend to do what we want to do. Please help us to see clearly the path you want us to take. When we stumble and fall please continue to pick us up. Help shake us off and put us in the right direction. Thank you for the talents you have given us. Let us use those to glorify you. In Jesus' name we pray,

Amen

Chapter 5

Leaving Hell Behind

When I think of hell, I think of my Aunt Kitty. But not in the way you would expect. In fact, Aunt Kitty is one of my all-time favorite relatives. When I was growing up, we always wanted to be with Aunt Kitty. She was the funny, outgoing aunt who knew all the crazy car songs. She has red hair, light green eyes and a great laugh. She is Catholic and I grew up Lutheran, so I didn't always know why she was making the sign of the cross or praying to Mary. But I respected her relationship with God. One day, she was upset about having to clean up cigarette butts that my Uncle Bill had left out. She made a remark about how she would spend her eternity in hell picking up cigarette butts. I asked her about it. Her theory was that if you went to hell, you would spend eternity doing what you hated most in life. That was your punishment. I was retelling this story at a party recently. My friend said they would be doing laundry. I replied, "Well, I would be running the nursery." Then my friend reminded me that children don't go to hell.

I got to thinking about the whole hell issue. I think people can put themselves in hell on earth. Just look at the news stories of people who get addicted to meth, or addicted to spending to the point where they have bill collectors hunting them down, or we surround ourselves with all our stuff so that we can't move in our own homes. That is a life without joy. I believe that is the front porch of hell. We all get caught up with the idea that we need stuff, usually because other people have stuff. Or we need to experience something strange and different to spice up our lives. I have seen people who have everything that you could possibly want but didn't have an ongoing relationship with God. They had no outlet of joy that comes from being part of something bigger than yourself. I have watched them crumble as things got tough. I have seen them turn against each other. I have seen them yelling at their kids because they couldn't handle any more pressure.

I don't care what religion you are. We all start with God. God offers us a way out. We are all his children. He doesn't want us to suffer like the prodigal son. He doesn't want us to make our own hell on earth. But there are some people who just don't believe that God's love for us is unconditional. He is the eternal optimist. He believes in us even when we don't. I know some of you are saying but we need to do good deeds to get into heaven, right? Not exactly; if you have a relationship with God, you talk to him, you get to know him and you share what you have learned. Then you will want to do good works, you will want to do his will, and the exciting part is that you will find joy in doing those things. Joy that no possession will ever give you. This comes from the same person who thought they would be running the nursery in hell. Now I am the Vacation Bible School Director and I can't even begin to tell you the tremendous amount of joy that gives me. It's not just the children either. My joy comes from the unexpected volunteers, the donations of supplies, the building of the teams, the decorations coming together and the eventual smiles of the children and their parents.

Part of celebrating life is finding joy and leaving hell's porch behind.

Chapter 6

Avoiding Big Inconveniences

When things don't go quite right, we want to blame someone, we want to know why things happened the way they happened. For me, I am trying to focus on the what. Instead of saying, "Why did Aunt Marguerite have to die from breast cancer?" I am saying, "What does God want me to learn from this event, from this person?" It takes awhile to make the switch. But once you do it, it really opens up the conversation and truly, positive does come from negative. For instance, because of my Aunt Marguerite and my mother and Aunt Barbara who also had breast cancer, I have been on the ball with my mammograms. So two weeks ago when I had my mammogram and they had me meet with a doctor instead of letting me put on my shirt and go, I already knew the reason.

They had detected something that could be nothing but they would rather find out. So I scheduled my biopsy a week later. The biopsy was not quite what I expected. I became concerned when the doctor told me that I would hear a small snap noise and instead I felt that I had been hit with a slingshot. The nurse tried to comfort me by rubbing a circle on my back while applying pressure. I lay there wondering why is she applying pressure? Did she get the signal from the doctor? We've got a jumper. I made it through the rest of the biopsy and wandered out wearing sunglasses into the lobby where my good friend Amy was waiting. I took her hand and she walked me past the various waiting areas towards parking. About halfway through, I said, "Great! First the anesthesia doesn't work .Now all of these people think we're dating."

It is a week later and now I am awaiting my results. So I hope you have learned at least two things from my experience: 1) always bring sunglasses to doctor's appointments and 2) bring a friend who has a good sense of humor. I decided not to look up anything about BC because I don't want to go there. If I have it, there will be plenty of time to look that stuff up. If I don't then I haven't lost any time. I know that I will not die from breast cancer but it would be such an inconvenience. I mean I have a busy schedule between working for my husband part-time, the kids and my volunteer work. There are some upsides of BC, like going shopping for wigs, losing weight and getting to lie around a lot. Imagine how many TV shows I could catch up on. I know how to knit. I could make myself plenty of scarves and hats. (OK, I know how to make scarves but no clue on hats. The last hat I made for my son was so uneven and the pom-pom fell apart. He looked like a poster boy for one of those starving nations in a cold environment.)

My kids and I play "Worst Case Scenario." Not the board game, but our own little "What happens if" game. For instance: on the first day of school, my son Michael was nervous. It was his first day in 6th grade. So he got my attention by saying, "I have a feeling that today is the day the world is going to end." (I should preface this by letting you know that he watches way too much science and history shows on TV.) My response was, "Well, if the world ends, we all die and we will all go to heaven and hang out there." "Oh, OK," he said. Then he followed it up with, "I have a feeling that a satellite is going to fall from space and land on me." "Well," I said, "In the unlikely event that a satellite does fall on you, then you will die, go to heaven and we will see you later." A couple of minutes later the hyperventilating began. Don't worry. He did make it to his first class. I checked on him at lunch and he was fine.

I finally heard back from doctor's office. I got the call at 4:30 in the afternoon while the boys and I were at Roma Pizza eating an early dinner and catching up on homework. Good news! I don't have cancer--just some fibrous tissue. So I have a check up in six months. Phew!

Now I can email my women's Bible study group whom I asked to pray for me. I can continue my work on directing Sunday School.

Even with the joy of knowing that I don't have to deal with BC today, I know there is a good chance that I will have it one day because of my family history. However, I am not going to spend an ounce of time worrying about it. As they say, "Been there, done that, wrote the book." But I also know I am one of the fortunate ones who received the happy call today.

My mom once worked in an OB/GYN office as a physician's assistant. She told me about this beautiful, well dressed woman who had come into the office. The woman knew something was wrong but had been too afraid to do anything. By the time she disrobed, my mom was shocked that the cancer had blackened her breast and there was an awful smell as the cancer had eaten away at the live tissue. I am sorry to be so gory, but it just broke my mother's heart to see this beautiful woman who had let vanity and anxiety keep her from getting help.

I used to be a stockbroker in the 90's. I often counseled people on how to plan financially for their future. At least once a week I would meet with someone who wanted to retire in a couple of years.

Sadly most of them hadn't saved nearly enough to go into full retirement or any kind of retirement. They had put off learning more about what they needed to do because it was overwhelming to them. And by doing so they had made their situation very overwhelming indeed.

When I was a broker with J.C. Bradford & Company, I published an article called, "Don't Play Possum with Your Finances." The article was meant as a wake-up call to look at your finances and your life and do something proactive.

The point I am trying to make is that to check on your finances or to get your mammograms done is a small inconvenience compared to the big inconvenience of not being able to retire, losing your house because you didn't plan for emergencies, or going through extreme chemo because the cancer has grown to stage four. I can tell you from the experience of having gone through antiviral therapy (which is like a low dose chemo) that it will knock you on your butt and take your energy faster than you can make it. So take a minute and pray about your life and what have you been avoiding. What do you need to take care of so that you can continue to celebrate life?

Quick Prayer

Dear Heavenly Father,

Thank you for this day and everyone since the day you brought me into this world. You know what I have been avoiding. You know what needs to be done. I pray that you would give me courage and strength to take the next steps, to make the tough decisions and to stay the course.

I am weak and you are strong. Please continue to hold me up as I struggle. Please surround me with those who would encourage me in the right way. In your name, I pray.

Amen

Here is a reprint of the article:

Investment Update by Kim Ponce, Investment Broker Third Quarter 1997

When It Comes to Your Finances, Don't Play Possum

Living in Middle Tennessee, I can truly say that I have something in common with everyone no matter your wealth, religion or educational background. We have all seen our share of dead possum on the road.

The opossum with its night vision and climbing skills has a major problem with its natural defense system. When an opossum gets scared and overwhelmed by fear, it faints, appearing to be dead. This probably worked well for the opossum before so many people started driving at night. Nowadays it is pretty typical for an opossum to be crossing the road, see the headlights of an oncoming car and faint. The problem is they don't wake up in time to get out of the way of the next oncoming car and . . . squish.

I have spoken to many people who when dealing with their finances and investment choices felt so overwhelmed they did nothing. The problem with doing nothing is that you are leaving yourself in the middle of the road waiting for the next financial crisis or life changing event to hit. That's not much of a defense. Let's look at why you have avoided dealing with your finances and investment choices.

1) I don't know where to start.

Start with a piece of paper and a pen, make a list of what is important to you (i.e. goals like retirement, college funding, a trip to Hawaii, a new car or boat, being a millionaire, etc.) Once you have listed your goals look at your resources: checking account, savings account and any other financial information you may have.

2) I don't know what I am doing.

Remember, this is your money; you worked hard to earn it. Why wouldn't you take some time to make sure you have it when you need it? There are numerous ways to find out more information: classes, free seminars, reading books or magazines on the subject, meeting with a financial or investment advisor.

3) I don't have time to fool with it.

Dealing with your finances and investment choices does not have to be a full-time job for you. But it is important to take some time each month or each quarter to evaluate if you are on track towards your goals.

4) I don't like change.

Most people don't and that is why it is important to take the time to set things up right in the first place. You also want to review from time to time to make sure that your objectives are being met. One of the most common stories I hear is, "I was working with my best buddy from college who worked for this bank, and he's left the bank and the new guy never returns my calls." If you are working with a professional on your financial matters, it is very important that you feel comfortable with this person and your options that are available. This person could have the best intentions in the world but if their only options for you are a money market fund paying 4 percent or a one-year CD paying 5.75 percent ythen you may want to check around.

5) I'm not good at budgeting.

Setting up a strict penny for penny budget rarely works. However, knowing what monies are coming in and what monies are going out will help you realize if there is waste, or if you should pay off some debts early.

6) I don't want to take risks.

By doing nothing you are taking incredible risks. You are not planning for inflation, taxes or an emergency fund. This reminds me of the person who puts $10,000 in their mattress for ten years and takes it out only to be surprised that prices have gone up and they can't buy as much with it.

7) You fill in the blank _____.

My advice to you is to make a plan for yourself that is doable and don't play possum with your finances and investments that you have worked so hard for.

Side Note: This article was a big hit at the office, where some people started to call me possum to my chagrin. However, that all came to a stop one Friday afternoon when they called me to the office manager who had everyone gather around as he asked if I was familiar with a country singer by the name of George Jones. I said, "Yes."

Well, George Jones has been called Possum for years. One of the brokers went to see him and they brought back an autographed picture of George Jones which read, "Dear Kim, There's only room for one possum in this town. George Jones." Everyone had great laugh but I was happiest about not being called possum anymore.

Chapter 7

Mistakes

Alright, I will tell you the infamous Jr. Mint story. I was driving young Alex, who was not quite a year old, across town to Gymboree. I live on the less expensive side of town and no one has figured out that we need a Gymboree play place over here. Michael Augustus had been dropped off at Mother's Day Out. So I am spending my precious time driving forty minutes across town to make sure that Alexander does not miss out on this highly educational experience. Major guilt at work because I used to take his brother every week. Of course, that was when it was only twenty-five minutes away and I was desperate to leave the house to have human contact.

OK, so I am driving along about twenty-five minutes into the trip, and I glance in the back mirror Alex is asleep in his car seat. I then notice the bag from Dollar Tree on the floor next to me that still has not been unloaded from the car. Yesterday, I was in Dollar Tree and saw those big boxes of movie candy for only a dollar. What a bargain! I had to buy two. So now that I am the only conscious one in the car, I reach for the bag and grab out the Jr. Mints. I don't want to get chocolate on my hands so I open the box and pour a couple in my mouth every so often and then more frequently. Well, unbeknownst to me is the fact that some of the Jr. Mints, ever so light, have fallen into my lap, rolled down between my legs and are on my seat. I continue to enjoy my secret snack until we reach the mall. I even sit in the seat flipping through a catalog for awhile since I arrived early. OK, the mall is beginning to open. I open the car door and get out when what should I see out of the corner of my eye but a big brown mess on the seat of my car. "Oh no!" I think,"What is that?" I recognize it as the Jr. Mints which have become the Jr. Mess. I am sure you can picture the warm gooey puddle on the light gray cloth seat. This is bad. But then it dawns on me I was sitting there. So I turn around and bend over and am trying to see my bottom in the side view mirror in the mall parking lot and sure enough, I have a matching story on my butt.

Thank goodness for those words of wisdom we store up. I suddenly remember my friend Ferial telling me that baby wipes get out anything. It is worth a try. So I grab my baby wipes and begin to scrub the seat. Sure enough ten baby wipes later, the chocolate is out. Hurray! But what to do about the seat of my pants? First I grab a wipe as I stand outside of the car and I am about to use the side view mirror when I realize just how disgusting this would look to any passersby. So I carefully get into my driver's seat not sitting down and pull down my pants, take them off and put them on my lap. I begin to scrub the crotch of my pants with diaper wipes. Meanwhile, two guys in the parking lot decide to stop and talk about seven feet from the car. I am silently praying, Please don't look, please go away. Eventually, one of them gets into the car next to me and drives away. Well, there goes my cover. I have gotten the stains out so now it just looks like I have wet my pants. I do not carry spare pants but I did have a sweatshirt in the car. So I shimmy back into my refreshing pants and tie a sweatshirt around my waist, wake up my child and head into the mall play area where I promptly get out my cell phone and call my sister Merrie (who laughs hysterically the whole time.) I head on to Gymboree.

One week later, I get a call from Merrie and she says, "You are not going to believe this but I did the same thing with a Twix bar, only I was wearing white pants."

Ah the humility! So now you know I am less than halfway perfect. But the good news is that I am working on it. I believe that all things are possible through Christ, through our Father in Heaven. But I also believe that you have to take responsibility for your actions on earth. If you pray to be skinny but then you chow down at the all–you-can-eat pizza buffet, piling up extra desserts what do you expect. God has given us free will to choose right from wrong. We make mistakes all of the time that is how we learn. Haven't you told your kids that? I believe we are the teenagers in God's kingdom. Can you imagine the conversation, "God, I want a new car. Can you give me a new car?" asks the teenage us. "No. But if you work hard, save up your money, you will eventually be able to buy a car," says the heavenly father. We respond in a whining tone, "But God, you are our Dad, you're supposed to take care of us. You're supposed to give us stuff to help us succeed. Do you want me to be a failure? I thought you cared about me. I thought you loved me." I can imagine God shaking his head, "I do love you. I will always love you. I have showed you the way you need to go."

Nowhere in the Bible does God promise us a million dollars, a new car, a perfect spouse and two and half children. But he does show us how to live. Sometimes we get confused and we may not see the clear way to go. During those times you can consult the manual: The Bible. We know we are not supposed to be lazy, greedy or boastful. It says so in the Bible in 2 Corinthians 13:4-7, "Love is patient, love is kind. It does not envy, it does not boast, it is not proud. It is not rude, it is not self-seeking, it is not easily angered, it keeps no record of wrongs. Love does not delight in evil but rejoices with the truth. It always protects, always trusts, always hopes, always perseveres." The Bible makes the case that God is love. He loves us all the time and he wants us to love each other. According to Romans 13:10, "Love does no harm to its neighbor. Therefore love is the fulfillment of the law."

Quick prayer

Dear Heavenly Father,

We have messed up. We have been ungrateful. We have whined like small children. Thank you for loving us even when we are hard to love. Allow us to learn from our mistakes. Please forgive us for our unloving ways. Please help us to be a blessing to others. In your name we pray,

Amen

Chapter 8

Removing Roadblocks

What are successful Christians? Do they look different? Perhaps you see their heavenly glow as they come through the door. Where do they live? Can you tell their houses from the pearly gates when you come up the driveway? Are they tall or short, do they have athletic bodies? I think that success in the real world is defined by achieving certain steps, certain goals, by finishing seven step programs. But how can we tell if we are successful as Christians? Can you imagine the typical speaker at a seminar asking the crowd, "Have you brought someone closer to God, helped someone reach out to Jesus?" I can just see the nice looking older couple in the corner. The man raises his hand. The woman elbows him, causing his arm to drop, as she hisses, "Almost running over someone doesn't count!" There is some truth there. We tend to seek out God when we are in trouble, when we are in danger, when we are overwhelmed beyond our capabilities.

So what is Christianity? Is it like being Italian? Are you are born with it? I wonder sometimes if that is what the bench warmers think. You know the people who come to service pretty regularly but think the one hour a week is all they have to put into it. What do you think it means to be Christian? Once you are baptized and confirmed are you set for life? Set for life until that trouble or danger comes along. Wouldn't that make God the Maytag repairman of heaven? We have all seen the commercials, where the poor Maytag repairman sits lonely in his office because no one has called in for a service call because the Maytags are so good. Is life so good that you don't need God anymore? At least not until something breaks down in your life. Is this the kind of relationship that you want with your heavenly Father? I hope not.

I am guilty of this behavior myself. Once I was in college I neglected my relationship with God. I never doubted his power. I never doubted my faith. I just allowed a lot of other people, places and things to crowd my mind. When I was home from college on a long weekend, I would go to church with my family, but I would go right back to college and he would once again be out of sight, out of mind. Sad, isn't it? The good news is I came back, just like the prodigal son. And not so surprising--God was still there.

I am not a theologian. I am merely a woman with a great faith in the only God I know. I believe in the Trinity--the powerful relationship of God the Father, Jesus the Son and the Holy Spirit. For me, what I keep hearing over and over again when I read the Bible is that God loves us. He loves us as his children. He wants us to learn from him, to behave like him. And that is where it gets confusing. Do we go with an eye for and eye as in the Old Testament? Or if we are slapped, do we turn the other cheek so that we may be slapped again? Is that what it is like for God, when we get upset and yell, "I hate you, God!" Aren't we slapping him with our verbal assault? Yet he readily forgives us when we are done with our tantrums.

It is my understanding that the Old Testament means the old covenant or what we would call agreement. So that would make the New Testament the new agreement. Once again it gets confusing. I have recently felt a new desire to study the Bible more thoroughly. Is this the nudge of God? Let's see . . . would he want me to get to know him better? Yes. Would he want me to learn more of his word so that I am more knowledgeable? Yes. So this must be the way he wants me to go. I realize not all ideas are so easy to discern. But let's face it--sometimes God's way is obvious.

Road Blocks

Politics: I think a big problem occurs when we mix our faith with politics. Don't get me wrong, I believe we should stand up for what we believe in. I see the problem when people choose sides because of politics: when they decide their political party or their group is the true word from God and the rest are heathens; that can lead you down an elitist path that gets very narrow indeed. If you take a political party's stand as your personal truth then you will be in constant confilct with your heavenly Father who says their is only one truth, God's truth. See, if God is love, and God wants you to love your neighbors, and care for one another and yet the politics you hold as truth tells you that you and your political beliefs are better than others then you have already begun to look down on others. To clarify in the Bible, God has always chosen the unlikely people to be lifted up, to deliver his messages, to guide his people: not the political leaders, the most popular or the most pious. For example, when Christ was born, he notified the shepherds who were considered to be pretty low on the food chain. Remember, they spent their time in the fields with sheep all day. They probably smelled ripe and looked dirty. But an angel of the Lord appeared to them to let them know that Christ was born. God's people were being terrorized and he sent a boy named David only armed with a slingshot to take out the giant Goliath. You must look for the good in all people not just those within the party.

Lack of Skills

Some people blame their lack of participation in God's work on their lack of skills. What can I do? I am not good at that. So what are these people going to do with their lives? Are they simply going to lie down and be the stones for others to walk on? I think if God ran a wanted ad, it might look like this:

Wanted: No experience necessary. Applicants must be willing to love others and attempt to do their best wherever they are needed. Lazy, self-absorbed, lying hoarders should also apply. Employer is willing to do on the job training. Great retirement benefits.

God does not want us to be perfect in order to have a relationship with us. He is willing to work with us. And so are his people. Both churches and non-profits are always looking for volunteers for various areas of service. So don't wait for the perfect moment or a golden invitation. If you don't see something right away, just ask at church or at one of the local non-profits. If it doesn't work out that is OK. I am sure that you are needed somewhere else. The world will never run out of opportunities to help. I need more evidence.

For me, having faith is like breathing. I have always had it, so it is part of me. I was very sick as a child and hospitalized often. My church family prayed for me often and each time I came through. So I have always known about God and God's power. But this is not the case for everyone. For some they have not been exposed to or given information about God when they were children. Or they were but something happened to make them question God and no one was there with the answers. I am not going to pretend I have all of the answers. But you certainly don't get anywhere unless you make an effort. There are a great many books that can help people make a connection. There are people out there who can answer questions you may have, and of course God is always there if you are willing to listen.

Quick Prayer

Dear Heavenly Father,

Thank you for your blessings that you have given us. Please help us to identify the road blocks that would keep us from you and help us to remove them or get around them. In your name we pray.

Amen

Chapter 9

Intentional Kindness

In the movie, *Evan Almighty*, actor Morgan Freeman plays the role of God. In the final scene he lets Evan know that ARK stands for Acts of Random Kindness. For awhile there was some mention of people doing acts of random kindness. It got some news time.

Recently, I have been reading a lot of books about God and different theories on what we are supposed to be doing, what God is doing and what is supposed to happen here on earth. While the books are on varied subjects there has been a common theme. God didn't send Jesus so that we could put up a tree and keep the retail economy going. God not only wants us to do for others but he also nudges us in that direction. Of course, because we have free will many of us choose to ignore these nudges. That is where the problem lies.

I think it starts with kindness, not random, but intentional kindness towards others. If you were surrounded by people who always remembered your birthday, never missed saying thanks even for the little things, offered you a shoulder to cry on and an ear to listen to, you would feel loved. God and Jesus are about love. Imagine if everyone in the world showed kindness to each other. There would be no need for wars. People wouldn't starve to death. Crime would go down. I mean how many times have you seen one of those crime documentary shows where they look at the criminal's horrible childhood and blame that for his beginning.

It is my opinion that all of us need to start a campaign of kindness to everyone, not just the ones who support our cause or live in our neighborhood. I had started on a thank you mission a couple of weeks ago. I wrote several thank you notes to people who were helping me out by teaching Sunday School. Then I remembered these two ladies who always help out in the kitchen and I wrote them thank you notes too. So few people write thank you notes anymore. Sad. A thank you note is one of the easiest notes to write. If you don't know what to say, just thank them for their time, their effort, or their wisdom. I keep all of the thank you notes that I receive. This year I plan to make a scrapbook album of the thank you notes. So when I am having a bad day, I can just open the book and remember that my efforts are worth it.

As good as my thank you mission was, I felt that it wasn't enough and then I realized I had it all wrong. Allow me to explain:

My husband woke up the other morning and told me he had a dream in which I was killed by gunfire. But in the dream he went back in time and saved me. He said that in the dream I was so thankful that I snuggled up to him like I did when we were first married. I was overjoyed to have him in my life. I couldn't shake this conversation. I started to realize that we had started to talk to each other like employees. We were forgetting to even look each other in the eyes. It has been more than twenty years since we started dating but I remember the excitement we had for each other and for life. I could make up excuses, "Well, we had kids and bills and life got in the way." But you see that doesn't matter. If I am to succeed in God's plan of kindness and love to all than I have to start out at home.

So I have been working on intentionally being kinder, more respectful and more loving to my husband, who is really the best husband in the world. I am trying to remember to thank him for loading the dishes even though I do the job 80 percent of the time. He in turn is trying to remember to compliment me if the kitchen looks picked up versus the dirty plate explosion of late. We are showing respect, kindness and love to each other more readily. And it is lovely.

So now I am ready to take on the world with kindness and love. The only problem is I don't know where to start first. Should I save the animals, save the earth, feed the people in poor countries, feed the people in this country? It can get overwhelming. On a positive note there is no shortage of needs and you could probably start anywhere. But should you? Take a moment now and say a prayer. Ask God to guide you to where you are needed right now. Ask God to show you what to do. Now you may not hear a deep voice or see a large cloud appear. But if you keep your eyes and ears open to opportunities to help others, you will start seeing areas where you can help.

Just to recap for those of us with short attention spans, showing kindness and respect is showing love. We need to start at home showing love to our family. We should thank people any chance we get. Lastly, we need to take our love out into our neighborhoods and the world to make a difference.

Below are some inspirational quotes on Neighbors from the NIV Bible:

Leviticus 19:16

> Do not go about spreading slander among your people. Do not do anything that endangers your neighbor's life. I am the LORD.

Leviticus 19:18

> Do not seek revenge or bear a grudge against one of your people, but love your neighbor as yourself. I am the LORD.

Proverbs 3:28

> Do not say to your neighbor, 'Come back later; I'll give it tomorrow'--when you now have it with you.

Matthew 25:35-40

> For I was hungry and you gave me something to eat, I was thirsty and you gave me something to drink, I was a stranger and you invited me in, I needed clothes and you

clothed me, I was sick and you looked after me, I was in prison and you came to visit me.

Then the righteous will answer him, "Lord, when did we see you hungry and feed you, or thirsty and give you something to drink? When did we see you a stranger and invite you in, or needing clothes and clothe you? When did we see you sick or in prison and go to visit you?"

The King will reply, "I tell you the truth, whatever you did for one of the least of these brothers of mine, you did for me."

Romans 13:10

Love does no harm to its neighbor. Therefore love is the fulfillment of the law.

Quick Prayer

Dear God in Heaven,

Thank you for sending Jesus to show us how to treat each other. Help me to bring your heaven to earth. Help me to spread joy and kindness to all not just those I know. Thank you for patience with my efforts. Thank you for the friendships that I have made. You have blessed me; please allow me to be a blessing to others.

Amen

Chapter 10

Welcoming One and All

I believe this may be one of the easiest but most often forgotten social skills. To welcome someone into your home, into your church, into your family, into your heart is to say I accept you the way you are and I am glad that you are here. I recently made the startling realization that I was chubby. Now, I know this would not startle many people. But I had been slowly gaining weight, which also meant that my wearable wardrobe was shrinking. So I began to look for weight loss options. Luckily, I had posted my anguish over finding a place to work out on my Facebook. My neighbor Lori commented that she taught a low impact class on Monday –Wednesday- Friday and it was cheap and fun. So I thought, OK, I will give it a try.

So Monday morning, I showed up in my t-shirt and hideously ugly workout shorts. I didn't realize how ugly they were until I saw my whole ensemble in the mirrored room. But I decided I would let it be an incentive instead of a devastating moment. Well, Lori was already there. She immediately smiled and greeted me. She introduced me to each of the ladies there. "This is my neighbor Kim. Kim this is Betty she goes to Connell." I felt welcome right away. Some other ladies arrived later. She greeted each one by name and then introduced me as well. If it hadn't been for Lori and her good-natured welcoming spirit, I could have just as easily have slunk off never to return after noticing everyone in the class was in better shape than I was. (I was the youngest and in the worst shape.) But instead I felt encouraged by the sharing of her joyful spirit. Everyone in class seemed uplifted to be there.

I confess I am terrible at memorizing people's names. I am great at remembering stories but for some reason I really struggle with people's names. One year I realized that I may not be the only one. So I began to use name tags at parties. It is a great investment when you have a big group. Also, some people may only see each other once a year, so having name tags helps everyone to welcome each other. Another thing that I do to help people feel welcome in my house is I clear out the coat closet. Rather than making everyone traipse upstairs to a guest bedroom with their coats, I can open the hall closet, reach in for a hanger and hang their coast. It is another small way to make people feel that they belong there.

Taking the time and effort to make sure that there are drinks and some kind of light snack is also important if you want people to feel comfortable and stay for awhile. It doesn't have to be anything fancy. My church has a small assortment of breakfast type snacks as well as coffee each Sunday between the services. We call it second breakfast in my house. Second breakfast made my children feel comfortable about switching to St. Tim's. In fact, after a couple of weeks of attending, I asked them if they wanted to go back to the other church for a Sunday. But they both said, "No". They said they felt welcome.

I felt welcome because of the four people I knew there. All of them greeted me at the first service that I attended. Over the next couple of months I was invited to join a Sunday School class, a women's Bible Study and help out at VBS. After that I hinted that I liked reading when I heard about a Book Club some of the members went to. I was invited to that too. I found a church home at St. Timothy and my kids did too. What a blessing being welcomed is!

I take great pride in welcoming family when they come to visit. I do this on purpose. I want them to return and visit often. So I try to make things pleasant. I get my house cleaned. I research different events. I come up with an itinerary of things that we can do once they get here. I take them out to dinner or have one of their favorite meals at the house on the day they arrive. My children make big welcome banners. They can't help but feel that their presence is desired.

No one wants to make the effort to travel to a family member's house and throw their stuff down on an unmade bed, use a dirty bathroom and have to wonder if they are supposed to feed themselves. If you have had one of these experiences, no doubt you have also been left to watch television for hours for lack of a better plan. When this happened to me, I thought, I can watch television at home. So I found a computer and looked up things we could go and do and presented them to my host, who agreed they sounded good. And off we went. You do have to realize as a guest that not everyone finds it easy to host other people or to even know what to plan. I think you just need to be willing to try.

Welcoming children is something I specialize in. As VBS director, I want every child to feel welcome in our church. I work countless hours to line up the right guide with each group of children. I make sure the snacks are children friendly. I make sure the games are action packed. I make sure the crafts are fun, something they would be happy to bring home. I make sure that every day they have a small token that not only reminds them of the lesson but is useful. (I am not a fan of Bible Buddies [little plastic characters]). I find they get lost in the bottom of the toy box.

It is a lot of work but when you see the children happy, learning and ready to come back the next day to find out more about God, it is totally worth it.

You can make your volunteers feel welcome by having nice nametags for them. You can provide special snacks for them. You can have silly awards at a pizza banquet. Always give them thank you notes. One thing I like to do for my volunteers is to ask local businesses to donate freebies: for example, a coupon for a free ice cream, or a free chicken sandwich, etc… The volunteers enjoy the little bonus and it doesn't cost any money out of budget.

So if you want to make people feel welcome, remember to greet them with a smile on your face and look them in the eyes. If there are other people around, introduce them. Have a small snack and drink available because people find comfort in food. Thank people for coming to you or your event. Let them leave with a smile and the knowledge that their presence was desired and you accepted them for themselves.

As I began to write this chapter, it suddenly occurred to me: Are we ready to welcome God into our homes, our lives, our heart? Have we made up our itinerary to spend time with him? Have we set a place for him at our table? Are our children ready with their welcome signs?

Quick Prayer

Dear Heavenly Father,

Thank you for welcoming us into your family. Thank you for blessing us so that we may share our blessings with others. Help me to welcome others, to share joy and to be a blessing. Please forgive me for the times that I have rushed past and missed opportunities to do so. With your help, I will keep my eyes open for opportunities to welcome others.

In your name we pray,

Amen

Epilogue:

Today (Spring Break 2010)

You will be happy to know that I am still around and looking quite healthy, I might add. Most of all, I want to let you know what I did with all of that knowledge God shared with me during my experience. I became more involved at church. I attended a Bible Study called Experiencing God. That study helped direct me to look for where God was already at work and to see what I could do to help. I felt God calling me to work with children as I worked as a substitute teacher. I started helping teach Sunday school class for the fourth through fifth grades. I thought that I should go back for my master's and become a teacher. So I started getting information together. I called for catalogs from the universities. I even met with the staff at David Lipscomb University. But it seemed like every path towards getting certified as a teacher had a roadblock. During this time, my friend Monica asked me to direct Vacation Bible School at my church. I said I would think about it.

One night when I was so frustrated with the certification not working out. I prayed to God. I said, "God I thought you wanted me to become a teacher but nothing is working out. What do you want me to do?" A couple of minutes later, it dawned on me that the teacher idea was mine, the working with children idea was his. That is when I remembered being asked about directing VBS, something I had never done before. This was January, two years after I had started my treatment. I emailed my friend Monica who had asked me to do this. I told her all about my prayer and she was excited that I was going to do it.

I have to tell you. I had the best time planning out VBS and directing it. I had so much fun that I asked to do it again. My church said yes. That is what joy is. It is the amazing feeling you get from doing something for the Lord that you love. It puts a smile on your face and your smile radiates to all those around you.

My husband and I will be celebrating our eighteenth anniversary this year. His law practice has continued to grow even though the economy has pulled back. He has never lost a case in court and still chases the kids around the house pretending to be a mummy. Michael Augustus was second place this year at the Geography Bee at school. Alex was first place in the school 5K race as well as having very good grades. I have a sink full of dishes to get to, so I will be off. But before I go, remember--smile every chance you get, don't wait for someone to ask you to help out and remember children absorb more than you will ever know, so love them like God would.

Love,

The Queen of Lemonade

Appendix A

I. How to throw a World Peace Dinner Party

My favorite party of the year is my World Peace Dinner Party. For years my family has asked me what I want for Christmas only to roll their eyes when I responded, "world peace." Ever since I was a little girl and rode the "It's a Small World" ride at Disney World, other cultures and lands have always fascinated me. I used to love to see dolls from around the world with their different costumes.

So one year, after listening to my husband complain for the hundredth time that we never use our dining room table for dining, I made a decision. Instead of our typical 'bring an appetizer' Christmas party, we would invite the same amount of people and ask them to bring an international dish to share. The dish could be something they grew up with at Christmas or something they wished had been served at Christmas. I was asking a lot from my friends, so I figured the turnout would probably be lighter.

I figured wrong. About ten days before the party I had sixteen people who had RSVP'd . . . then twenty-eight . . . soon thirty-six people. By the day before the party we had forty-eight people who were coming for dinner. And fifty showed up. I borrowed tables and chairs from my good friend Patty. We had tables in every room of the house. I had one pulled up to my couch in the den, one pulled up to the piano bench in the living room; the rec room was packed with tables too. I had wine and water on every table with real wine glasses and thick paper plates. There was a soda bar in the kitchen. Each wine glass had a flag from a different country so people could tell their glasses apart. I had purchased extra silverware at the local Sam's Club and some inexpensive white restaurant tablecloths.

Once everyone had gotten settled in, I asked each table of participants to say grace and then they could go through the buffet line. It was slow going but the food was so worth it. After most of the people were finished, I asked the guests at the folding tables to clear their own tables and set the folding table in the rec room against the wall. Everyone did. Then we played an ornament exchange game. Next, everyone was invited for desserts, which were set up buffet style in the dining room while we began to sing Christmas songs.

The cleanup was easy. Everyone brought the food. So I only had one dish and a bunch of wine glasses to wash. I even received thank you notes from some of my guests. The party allowed everyone to try some different foods that they might not have tried otherwise. I think that is part of the key to world peace. When we are willing to get to know one another and each other's cultures, we develop an appreciation for our differences. Besides, this is more fun than working at the UN

Inviting

The best way to plan this one is to make up your guest list early. Pick a Saturday night versus a Friday night when everyone is busy heading home from work. Send invites out at least three weeks in advance. Your invitation should specify that guests need to bring an international dish, contact you to tell you what they are bringing and start calling for sitters early. This is more of an adult party. Don't be afraid to borrow tables and chairs. You may want to co-host this party with a friend. You can use disposable plastic cups and cutlery.

Seating

I don't assign seats so that my friends are forced to sit with other people they don't know well. I also provide nametags and a sharpie on each table. If you have shy friends, you could have a little conversation starter list on each table: What is your favorite Christmas song? Holiday foods?

. . . Did your family have a special Christmas tradition? . . . Favorite gift as a child, etc. I would also try to encourage people to fill one table up at a time to keep guests from sitting by themselves at a table waiting for someone to find them. When possible I try to introduce guests who don't know each other and point out something they have in common. As host you wait till everyone has found a seat and then sit in an unoccupied seat. I will tell you that some people are terrible about canceling at the last minute. When possible remove place settings as people cancel. Always leave at least two extra settings, in case a set of your guests surprise you, which happened to me. If not for my extra settings, my husband and I would have been eating over the sink.

To Wine or Not to Wine

You don't have to provide wine. The reason I had wine and water on each table was to keep people seated. You can imagine the kitchen is already hectic with people bringing in their special dishes and setting them up. You could easily substitute a soda or wassail (if it is cold outside), which is delicious. Wassail, for those of you who don't know, is a traditional English drink served hot. Southern Living had a great recipe, which I adopted years ago that uses three types of juice and frozen lemonade then it is heated with cinnamon sticks and orange slices with cloves in the skin of the orange. Yum. It smells and tastes delicious.

Dinner Is Served

Once most of the people are there (by most I mean you are only missing one to three couples), then begin letting one table at a time go through the line. I suggest walking around chatting with various tables so you can keep an eye on the line. I found that by asking them to say grace first, it eliminated a wild animal rush to the kitchen. There should be plenty of food. Some dishes will be gone by the time you get through the line, seeing as you are at the last table. But believe me, there will be more than enough. Once every table has gone the first time, you can go from table to table and let your guests know that they can go up for seconds. This is the perfect time for you to eat your dinner and chat with your tablemates as the party is now on cruise control.

The Gentle Art of Clearing the Table

I have found that people will only sit for so long, especially in folding chairs, so you have to provide an exciting event to move on to. You also have to get rid of all these extra tables and chairs. My husband thought I was insane when I told him that I planned to ask each table of people to clear their plates, throw the table cloth in the laundry room and fold up the tables and chairs. But, you know what, they all did it and it gave us more room to roam. You will find that some guests will go on automatic pilot and begin retrieving their dish and packing it up. Some of my friends began washing wine glasses for me. I had to tell them to stop.

That's Entertainment

You don't have to have an ornament exchange. One year we all brought white elephant gifts to exchange. We use the rules where everyone draws a number. Each number is called in order. When your number is called, you get to pick out a gift that is still wrapped on the table or you may take an item that has already been unwrapped by someone else. I limit the taking of gifts to three times or you would be doing this all night. After the last person has chosen, the first person gets a chance to keep what he or she exchanges with someone else. Just remember: Never put an item in that you were given by one of the party participants, although you must put this information in the invite ahead of time. Also, it is best to limit it to one per household or you will be trading ornaments all night.   One year we held a talent show in the rec room. We had everyone bring the folding chairs in there and make rows. It was crowded but fun. I had found some knock-knock jokes on the Web. So I asked one couple to read them. I had a friend who sang. We made up a skit. I also looked up letters to Santa. I typed them up on slips of paper and they were distributed throughout the audience. As I called out the child's name, different members of the audience read the cards to Santa. It was very sweet. I had some guests who volunteered to play a song or sing. You could even host it as an event at your church. Also, if you have anyone who plays guitar, you could do a round of caroling and maybe even a reading of the Christmas Story. After that, enjoy dessert with your friends. It helps if you assign at least one friend to be in charge of making the coffee so you don't have to think about it. Desserts hopefully have made their way to a single table and can be accessed buffet style. And that is how you have a World Peace Dinner Party of your own.

II. How to Have a Life Is Sweet Party

I have hosted two Life Is Sweet Parties. One was to celebrate the halfway point in my treatment and the other was for my recent birthday. This is a much simpler party to have, and I think would be a wonderful thing to do for a friend who was at a halfway part or the end of a medical treatment. I also liked using it as the theme for my birthday party because I told my friends that they had blessed my life and I wanted to share my birthday with them. If you are doing a small party, you could opt for all desserts, fruit, cheese and crackers. If you are throwing it for a friend, you may want to divide up the food list with the guests who are coming so that you don't wind up with eight trays of brownies. I would serve with sparkling cider or a dessert wine. Put out the fancy glasses and cocktail party napkins to make it seem special. When displaying desserts, fancy trays, raised cake stands and doilies under the food always make the table appear prettier. A plain white tablecloth or some other festive cloth also makes the look complete. This could be a short two-hour party for a small group of friends.

If you want to do this on a bigger scale or for a longer amount of time, then you are going to need some appetizers to balance out all of the sweets. In that case, ask your guests to bring one or the other. Anytime I have a buffet table at a party, I put out a veggie tray to start. It helps to fill the table and it provides some raw nutrition to even out all of the buttery, cheesy, sugary food. This is a great way to have a party because everyone else brings the food and you just provide the place and the drinks.

As far as drinks go, I have found that most guests will go for a mixed drink in a pitcher. It doesn't seem to matter what it is, what color it is or whether it has alcohol or not. For some reason they are just attracted to "the made just for you "drink. You can make up the drink in a pitcher or a punchbowl. For alcohol, I usually purchase those big bottles of already made up mixed drinks from the liquor store and pour it over ice. If you want a non-alcoholic fun drink, try mixing Sprite or Sprite Zero with a citrus or tropical fruit juice. It looks pretty and it tastes great. You can even throw some fresh fruit in if you are feeling lucky. I would suggest pineapple, orange or maraschino cherries. Apples, bananas and regular cherries have no business floating in the punch.

So now you and your guests are feasting around the table munching on food. Do you need to do more or not? I think it is fun to have something going on. For my birthday, we played 'amnesia'. This is a game where you have the names of famous people on labels. As guests entered, my husband put a label on each guest's back. They then had to ask each guest only one question about whom they might be. This turned out to be fun and it forced some of my friends to meet other friends.

Another thing you can do for a grown-up birthday party, you can have a birthday girl/boy trivia contest. Simply come up with ten multiple-choice questions that your guests may or may not know about the birthday girl/boy. For those who wanted to play, I gave them each a pad of paper. I announced the question and gave the four possible choices. They secretly wrote down which answer they thought it was and I had them hold up their answers at the same time. This can be funny and it allows your guests to know a little bit more about the birthday girl/boy. Another take on this is to ask each guest ahead of time for a fact the other guests don't know about him or her. Then you type up all the facts and have them try to find out which guest goes with which fact. Who is 100 percent Swedish? Who was on the fencing team in high school? . . . etc. This is a great conversation starter.

Appendix B

Facts about Hepatitis C

When I was first tested for the quantity of the virus in my system in July of 2006, the number was over three million. In January when I started the antiviral therapy, my number was over four million. Normal is zero. So, essentially the treatment I was on was supposed to bring my number down to zero and then keep it that way. The test they use is only for blood. However, the virus also hangs out in your tissues. That is why it can come back. That is also why you start the treatment and once you get to zero you stay on it for an additional six months to get rid of any extra passengers.

Getting to Know Your Liver Better

So I gave it some thought today (at least 20 minutes) and decided to do some research. As I began to look up my options, I realized how little information I really knew about my liver and my disease. I figured if I know that little you might too. Oh, don't get me wrong, I know that some of you are geniuses. I mean, I really do. But you can just read this and let your non-genius friends know about it.

According to the Hepatitis Foundation International website:[1] "Your liver is about the size of a football, making it the largest organ in your body. It refines and detoxifies everything we eat, breathe and absorb through our skin. It is the internal chemical power plant, converting nutrients in the food you eat into muscles, energy, hormones, clotting factors and immune factors." Pretty handy, I would say. Apparently, it stores vitamins, minerals and sugars. It even controls the production of cholesterol. The main problem is that your liver doesn't send out pain signals when it is in trouble. That is why most people with a liver problem or hepatitis don't know they have it until they are tested or their disease has progressed to a severe stage.

How to Have a Happy, Non-Stressed Liver, According to My Research

1. Three Things to Avoid

In order to have a happy healthy liver, avoid drinking large quantities of alcohol. (Because alcohol is the only thing that they know damages the liver). You should also avoid taking acetaminophen (Tylenol) with the alcohol and environmental pollutants such as paint thinners, bug sprays, aerosol sprays, etc.

2. Achieve Balance

Now this next quote is for my friend Kathy and my dad. According to the Hepatitis Foundation website, "Poor nutrition is rarely the cause of liver disease." I was delighted with this extremely happy news wondering how many hot dogs, packs of Twizzlers, and Little Debbie snacks I could survive on. Yippee! Hurray! Oh I forgot to mention the rest of the quote. . . . "But good nutrition in the form of a balanced diet, may help liver cells damaged by hepatitis viruses to regenerate, forming new liver cells." Too much protein, too much carbs, too much salt and too much vitamin A are all bad for your liver. According to the Hepatitis Foundation website, "Too much daily protein can cause hepatic encephalopathy (mental confusion). This occurs when the amount of dietary protein is greater than the liver's ability to use the protein. This causes a buildup of toxins that can interfere with brain function." The article went on to say, "Eating too much carbs can cause fat deposits on the liver." Ewww! Excess Vitamin A can be toxic to your liver, according to the Hepatitis Foundation. Having too much salt can cause fluid retention, which causes the swelling of the abdomen or swelling of the legs.

What is Cirrhosis Really?

Cirrhosis is a condition in which normal, healthy liver cells are damaged and are replaced by scar tissue. Patients with cirrhosis often lead normal healthy lives for many years. Most of the side effects of the disease are treatable. However a cirrhosis-damaged liver can cause widespread disruption of many body functions." That is why some people with cirrhosis can have symptoms of fatigue, loss of appetite, nausea and vomiting, jaundice (yellowing of the skin and the whites of the eyes), formation of gallstones, accumulation of water in the abdomen, accumulation of water in the legs called edema, bruising and bleeding easily, enlargement of the liver and even itching caused by a buildup of bile products in the liver. On a side note, I don't have any of those side effects except the inflammation of the liver. Phew!

Can Cirrhosis Be Cured?

Not yet. But there are some drugs out there that can delay its progress. The above facts I found online at www.hepfi.org.

What is Hepatitis C?

According to WebMD,[2] "Hepatitis C is a virus that infects the liver. In time, it can lead to permanent damage of the liver, as well as cirrhosis, liver cancer and liver failure. Some people who are infected with Hepatitis C have it for a short time and then get better. This is known as acute hepatitis C." I have what is called chronic Hepatitis C, which is when the virus is long term.

What causes someone to develop a Hepatitis C infection?

Hepatitis C is spread from one person's infected blood to another person's blood. According to Web MD, "You can get hepatitis from sharing needles or other drug equipment to inject drugs or if you had a blood transfusion or organ transplant before 1992. They began screening blood for the virus in 1992. "You cannot get hepatitis C from hugging, kissing, sneezing, coughing or sharing food or drink."[7] That is how you get other stuff. But not hepatitis C, so I can sneeze and kiss all I want to. Many people live with the virus for twenty to forty years without becoming seriously ill. According to WebMD, "Symptoms of hepatitis C include fatigue, joint pain, belly pain, itchy skin, sore muscles, dark urine and jaundice."

How do you find out if you have hepatitis C?

Most people find out by accident, like I did, when they try to donate blood. They now offer a screening test you can purchase at some drug stores. Some people with Hepatitis will have high levels of liver enzymes (which I have never had). So if your doctor sees that, he may have you tested for hepatitis C antibodies to see if you have the virus. According to Web MD, "If the test shows that you have a high level of the virus antibodies, your doctor may suggest that you have a liver biopsy so they can get a small sample of your liver tissue to look for damage under a microscope."[9]

Current Treatment for the Hepatitis C Virus

According to Web MD, "Currently, the standard for treatment is antiviral therapy which is a combination of two medicines: peginterferon and ribivirin." Though there are drugs now going into trials, it will be several years before something new comes out. I have reviewed several noteworthy websites such as Web MD, the Mayo Clinic, the Hepatitis Foundation and none of them recommend herbal remedies at this point. There seem to be two reasons: some herbs can actually damage your liver and there haven't been enough comprehensive studies of how other herbal remedies work. Maybe someone or some institution will fund something soon. The exception is milk thistle, which has shown to help liver enzymes but not cure hepatitis C, which Dr. Mike confirmed.

Appendix C.

Financial Advice for Kindergartners

By Kim Ponce, a former investment broker*

#1) Don't invest in candy. It is easily eaten and then you have nothing left. Besides, people give you candy at Halloween and Easter just for looking cute.

#2) Choose wisely when spending your money. Really look at the toy you are about to buy. Is it sturdy or does it look like it will break easily?

#3) Sometimes, combining your money with someone else's to buy something is a good idea. But before you put your money in this partnership, make sure the person is a good sharer and your parents know what you have agreed to do.

#4) When you start saving money, tell your parents and grandparents about it. See if any of them will match what you are saving. (It doesn't always work but you can try anyway.)

#5) You can start earning money now. Just because you are a kindergartner, that doesn't give you an excuse. Look for dropped change inside the car or house with your parent's permission. Are there toys you no longer play with? Maybe you could sell them at a garage sale or consignment sale. Most of all, ask your parents and grandparents if there are any jobs that you can do to earn some extra money.

*Kim Ponce is a former investment broker with J.C. Bradford & Co. She no longer holds an investment broker license and cannot be paid for advice. Any and all of the information contained within is just common sense.

Source Citations

1. http://www.hepfi.org/living/liv_caring.html pages 1-2

2. http://www.webmd.com/hepatitis/hepc_guide/Hepatitis-c. topic overview pages 1-2